This book shows how the tools of improvisation can bring greater agility towards dealing with insecurity and complexity in working life. While mostly about handling virtual environments, you'll find reminders of truths that stay with us whether face-to-face or online, such as the value of co-creative cooperation.

Schinko-Fischli rightly puts the emphasis on interaction ahead of technology, noting for example the advantages of Zoom over other platforms in its offers of visibility of participants and welcoming breakout rooms. There are tips for increasing spontaneity and connection, such as inviting participants to keep their cameras and microphones on. And there's a good selection of games, ranging from the simplicity of word association to more complex forms such as invented birthday messages – and even suggestions to help us go beyond the screen, like connecting with a colleague via a mobile to take a reflective walk.

Paul Z. Jackson, author of *EASY: Your LIFEPASS to Creativity and Confidence and The Inspirational Trainer*

Learning Social Skills Virtually

Digital workshops and meetings have established a firm foothold in our everyday lives and will continue to be part of the new professional normal, whether we like it or not. This book demonstrates how workshops and meetings held online can be made just as interactive, varied and enjoyable as face-to-face events.

The methods from improvisational theatre are surprisingly well suited for online use and bring the liveliness, playful levity and co-creativity that are often lacking in digital lessons and meetings. Applied improvisation is an experience-oriented method that is suitable for developing all soft skills – online and offline. Alongside brief introductions to the most relevant themes, the book contains numerous practical exercises in the areas of teamwork, co-creativity, storytelling, status and appearance, with examples of how to implement them online.

This book, written in the climate of the COVID-19 pandemic, is important reading for everyone – coaches, professionals and executives – looking for new impulses for their digital workshops and meetings, and who would like to expand the variety of their online methods. It offers new perspectives on many soft skills topics and supports interactive, engaging, lively and profitable online learning.

Susanne Schinko-Fischli is a psychologist and actress and an expert in using applied improvisation to teach soft skills. She lectures at various universities in Austria and Switzerland and delivers training for companies such as IBM, Frequentis and Swisscom. She is also the author of the book *Applied Improvisation for Coaches and Leaders*, published by Routledge.

Learning Social Skills Virtually

Using Applied Improvisation to Enhance Teamwork, Creativity and Storytelling

Susanne Schinko-Fischli

Routledge
Taylor & Francis Group

LONDON AND NEW YORK

Cover illustration by Evi Fill

First published 2022
by Routledge
2 Park Square, Milton Park, Abingdon, Oxon OX14 4RN

and by Routledge
605 Third Avenue, New York, NY 10158

Routledge is an imprint of the Taylor & Francis Group, an informa business

British Library Cataloguing-in-Publication Data
A catalogue record for this book is available from the
British Library

Library of Congress Cataloging-in-Publication Data
Names: Schinko-Fischli, Susanne, 1972– author.
Title: Learning social skills virtually : using applied
    improvisation to enhance teamwork, creativity and
    storytelling / Susanne Schinko-Fischli.
Description: New York, NY : Routledge, 2022. | Includes
    bibliographical references.
Identifiers: LCCN 2021042614 | ISBN 9781032001074
    (paperback) | ISBN 9781032001104 (hardback) |
    ISBN 9781003172765 (ebook)
Subjects: LCSH: Social skills. | Teams in the workplace. |
    Creative ability. | Storytelling.
Classification: LCC HM691 .S44 2022 | DDC 302/.14—dc23
LC record available at https://lccn.loc.gov/2021042614

ISBN: 978-1-032-00110-4 (hbk)
ISBN: 978-1-032-00107-4 (pbk)
ISBN: 978-1-003-17276-5 (ebk)

DOI: 10.4324/9781003172765

Typeset in Times New Roman
by Apex CoVantage, LLC

Contents

Profiles   ix
   About the author ix
   About the illustrator x
Preface   xi
What you will find in this book   xiv

1   Applied improvisation   1

   1.1 Origin of improvisational theatre 1
   1.2 Introduction to applied improvisation 1
   1.3 Basics of improvisation 2
   1.4 Workshops with applied improvisation online 4

2   Creativity   12

   2.1 Introduction to (co-)creativity 12
   2.2 Creativity online 16
   2.3 Phases of the creative process 17
   2.4 Creativity and agility 18
   2.5 Exercises for creativity online 24

3   Teamwork   34

   3.1 Introduction to teamwork 34
   3.2 Teamwork online 37
   3.3 Exercises for teamwork online 42
   3.4 Improvised role-playing games online 48

4   Storytelling   50

    4.1 Introduction to storytelling 50

    4.2 Storytelling online 52

    4.3 Building stories 53

    4.4 The message of stories 57

    4.5 The Hero's Journey 59

    4.6 Using the Hero's Journey 60

    4.7 Exercises for storytelling online 62

5   Status and image   66

    5.1 Introduction to status behaviour 66

    5.2 Status online 69

    5.3 Status paradox 73

    5.4 Hierarchy paradox 73

    5.5 Appearance online 74

    5.6 Exercises for status online 76

    5.7 Exercises for appearance online 80

6   Practical examples   84

    Your takeaways from this book   100

    Literature   101

      Online sources   101

    Index   102

Profiles

About the author

Susanne Schinko-Fischli Susanne Schinko-Fischli, born in Vienna
in 1972, studied psychology at the University of Vienna and at the
University of California, San Diego. In addition, she underwent formal training in acting, and – alongside her work – she studied and
qualified as a group dynamics trainer. For many years, she took to
the stage with various improvisational theatre groups in Austria and
Switzerland. Since 2004, she has been an independent trainer with a

focus on and passion for the lively methods and dynamics of applied improvisation. Schinko-Fischli is a lecturer at the Universities of Liechtenstein and Graz, at the Zurich University of Applied Sciences, at colleges of applied sciences and at higher technical schools. As a trainer in the areas of social skills, teamwork, creativity and innovation, she works online and offline for well-known organisations in Switzerland, Austria, Germany and the English-speaking world. She is also the author of the book *Applied Improvisation for Coaches and Leaders*, published by Routledge in 2019.

About the illustrator

Evi Fill (Filluna) Evi Fill was actually a graphic designer, but whenever she ran out of images, she just drew them herself. Eventually, she switched to drawing and painting exclusively; however, she is still an advertiser at heart and works mainly for advertising agencies in Austria, Germany and Switzerland. She has been freelancing for ten years and enjoys the new challenges that brings.

Preface

On Tuesday, 10 March 2020, I went to a training seminar of the Austrian Society for Group Dynamics and Organizational Consulting in Lower Austria. I was travelling by train, passing through the snow-covered landscape of St. Anton am Arlberg. Outside there were still skiers on the slopes, the train was full and everything was very peaceful. The seminar took place in a cosy country inn in the Waldviertel, and in the evening, we all sat together as a group and had a good time.

On the Thursday evening, the situation suddenly changed. News and rumours came in on all channels, especially on social media. We became very nervous, and suddenly, it was completely uncertain whether it would be possible to drive home again after the seminar. We considered curtailing the seminar, but then decided we would stay together. The seminar was even more intense from that moment on and the last evening even more enjoyable and exuberant. In the meantime, the country inn had emptied, and on that last evening, it was just the staff and us in the restaurant. All bookings for the next few weeks had been cancelled.

On the Saturday afternoon, I started the journey home into the unknown – how the world had changed in these few days! Would I make it across the border back to Switzerland? The station in St. Pölten was ghostly empty – there was no one but me on the platform, and I was almost alone on the train. In Innsbruck, some stranded skiers got on . . . perhaps from Ischgl? In St. Anton am Arlberg, the train didn't even stop, and the connection to Switzerland was cancelled. I got off in Feldkirch and was lucky – my husband had been able to cross the border without any problems, and we made it back into Switzerland with no further trouble.

Our two sons had switched to homeschooling, and my husband and I were now doing home office. At first almost, all my bookings were cancelled, causing great shock and uncertainty. Fortunately, the first orders came back surprisingly soon – but online! Numerous course days had to be completely rescheduled, and the abilities of the technology discovered and tested.

Soon I started experimenting with improvisation online and moving to the virtual space the weekly training sessions with the improvisational theatre group I led. With very valuable previous experience, the online workshop with applied improvisation for the Austrian Research Promotion Agency (FFG) took place in May 2020, in cooperation with the Austrian University of Natural Resources and Life Sciences (BOKU). (See the chapter on practical examples.) The satisfaction of the participants was very high, just as with the face-to-face workshops. Gradually, the great potential of this medium for my work and my customers opened up.

As in my first book, *Applied Improvisation for Coaches and Leaders*, published by Routledge, this book is also about how the principles and methods from improvisational theatre can be used and implemented to train social skills. However, this new volume is specifically adapted for online workshops. The introductions to the respective topics incorporate important insights from the first book (Schinko-Fischli, 2019).

The present book begins with a general introduction to applied improvisation and the possibilities of using it online. The second chapter deals with the question of online communication of creativity and co-creativity. Improvisational theatre is at its core real teamwork and therefore offers a large pool of exercises that promote and strengthen team cohesion. Many of these "classic" exercises are also possible online. Another trending topic is storytelling within companies, and this can also be taught and practised very well online. The penultimate chapter, on status, deals with how linguistic and non-linguistic signals can have a major effect on our social influence. This concerns what social status we convey online, how we come across online and how we can learn to adapt our status behaviour to the situation at hand. In the last chapter, I go into more detail about three online workshops for different organisations and describe actual scenarios from these workshops.

Most chapters end with a collection of exercises for online use. Unfortunately, it is not possible to trace who originally developed which exercises. I got to know the exercises in workshops or by observing improv groups, discovered them in textbooks, or invented them myself and adapted them for online use. Many exercises go back to "old masters" such as Viola Spolin or Keith Johnstone.

This book is aimed at trainers, lecturers, teachers and coaches who are looking for new ideas and variety for their online work, and through applied improvisation, it offers a rich set of exciting and interactive methods for teaching social skills.

I would like to thank my husband Claudius Fischli very much for the support he has given me. From the very beginning, he encouraged me to write this book, offered me his suggestions and questions and enabled me to take several breaks so that I could reflect, research and write in peace.

Also, I want to thank John Newman for his great English translation; he always found the right tone and the best words.

And a big thank to Evi Fill for her unmistakable sense of "the idea behind the idea" and her wonderful illustrations.

Finally, I especially thank Susannah Frearson and Alexis O'Brien from Routledge for their inspiring and dedicated attention to this book, from the initial idea all the way to publication!

Susanne Schinko-Fischli
Appenzell, Switzerland, winter 2021

What you will find in this book

- How you can playfully impart social skills with applied improvisation.
- The value of the "Yes, and . . . " principle for co-creative collaboration.
- How to prepare people for co-creative collaboration online.
- How you can build cohesion, trust and openness in teamwork online.
- Which exercises from improvisational theatre you can use to create online workshops that are more interactive, lively and fun.
- How stories and "Heroes' Journeys" are structured and how you can use storytelling online to transfer knowledge or improve collaboration.
- The importance of our status behaviour and how we present ourselves in online meetings, how we can become aware of this and how we can change our status if we need to.

Chapter 1

Applied improvisation

1.1 Origin of improvisational theatre

The corona crisis of 2020 showed us how quickly our plans can be thrown to the four winds, and it tested whether, and how, we can deal with this. It certainly helps if we can improvise.

On stage, improvisation has been going on for a long time. In ancient times, it was simply because it wasn't possible to plan everything. At first, magical rituals and ceremonies were improvised. Texts and procedures began to become fixed only in late antiquity, and improvisation was ousted from the theatre. With the *commedia dell'arte*, improvisation flourished again in the theatre and was intensively used to criticise the social conditions of the time. It was only censorship that pushed back this form of the *Stegreiftheater* (improvised theatre).

Jacob Levy Moreno used the *Stegreiftheater* in his development of psychodrama in the 20th century, and other new forms of improvisational theatre emerged from that. Keith Johnstone developed Theatresports, which quickly spread throughout Canada, the United States and later Europe. Today, Theatresports and improvisational theatre are widespread almost all over the world, enjoying great popularity. The players improvise in shorter and longer formats, in response to suggestions from the audience.

1.2 Introduction to applied improvisation

In the 20th century, Jacob Levy Moreno wasn't the only one to experiment with how to use improvisational theatre off stage. Augusto Boal, for example, developed his "Theatre of the Oppressed" along similar basic principles, and Jonathan Fox developed "Playback Theatre." In 2002, the Applied Improvisation Network (AIN) was founded by Paul

DOI: 10.4324/9781003172765-1

Z. Jackson, Michael Rosenburg and Alain Rostain (http://appliedimprovisation.network), including annual conferences in the United States and Europe with participants from all over the world. The basic principles of this network can be summarised as follows:

- attention and contact
- non-verbal communication
- co-creation
- spontaneity and intuition
- a culture of trust that allows for mistakes

The methods of applied improvisation are becoming increasingly popular, particularly for continuing training. If agility and dealing with insecurity and complexity in working life are increasingly necessary, then the tools of improvisation offer excellent opportunities to expand these skills.

Since 2002, I have been working with the methods of applied improvisation in workshops, on the following topics:

- performance competence and presentation techniques
- communication
- creativity and innovation
- status and leadership skills
- storytelling
- team building

I have described these in more detail in my book *Applied Improvisation for Coaches and Leaders* (2019).

1.3   Basics of improvisation

To my mind, the following three basics form the core of improvisation:

Attention in the here and now

As in group dynamics or gestalt therapy, the "here-and-now" principle is of crucial importance in improvisational theatre. Because only when we're in the moment can we really listen to others. Only then can we perceive ourselves and others and react appropriately in the moment. As soon as we start thinking ahead and planning ahead, we easily miss the right instant and the right impulse. The improvised action is constantly co-designed on stage by all the participants and frequently changes direction. That's why co-creative work relies less on developing our own sophisticated ideas and more on letting go of our own concepts and ideas. As soon as we stick to our own ideas, we miss the moment and the joint development of new possibilities.

"Yes, and . . . " – accepting offers

The second basic rule when improvising is to accept offers: a "yes" takes up the offer, while the "and" develops the offer further. This is how co-creativity comes about! Incidentally, this also applies to our own ideas and impulses as we bring them into the world in the first place. There are many reasons why offers are so often blocked in everyday life. The most likely cause is trying to not allowing others to influence us or change us – in other words, control. Commitment and involvement do indeed require a certain amount of courage and self-confidence; in a sense, they represent a leap into the unknown, where the future is only developed as a joint venture along the way.

Making your partner look good ("let your partner shine")

The third improv principle is: make your partner look good. It's a wonderful tool for any successful teamwork. I would like to describe two experiences:

The first example is from a Zoom meeting with members from the AIN. The participants are spread all over the world, and one participant apologised for still being in her pyjamas. The host replied: "*It doesn't matter at all – on the contrary, it's an absolute must to take part in pyjamas!*"

I experienced my second example on the way back from an Applied Improvisation conference on Long Island. Several conference participants were sitting in the same train compartment. A colleague of mine was gushingly thanking another colleague for his great presentation during the conference. Then, it turned out that she had got him mixed up with someone else, which was embarrassing at first, of course. But another colleague immediately jumped in and told *me* that she would like to thank *me* for *my* wonderful lecture, which of course was not true, because she had not participated in any of my workshops. I, in turn, continued to play the game and thanked the next colleague for her brilliant presentation, and so on. Out of an unpleasant situation, a funny improv game had arisen.

1.4 Workshops with applied improvisation online

Before the corona crisis, I would never have dreamed that improvisational theatre online could be possible, let alone fun. But in the spring of 2020, it was all about "yes, and . . . " or no longer have any income . . . which definitely made the decision to get involved in this new professional adventure easier (Figure 1.1).

Figure 1.1 © Evi Fill

Technology

The videoconferencing tool "Zoom" (www.zoom.us) was helpful in the realisation of the initial ideas. It is very likely that there will be more providers with similar platforms in the future. The decisive factor with Zoom, however, was that you could see all participants (at least with a manageable group size) at the same time, as well as the possibility to run "breakout sessions." This made it feasible to work with groups methodically in a way that was quite similar to a normal face-to-face workshop.

An important function is that you can turn off your own camera and change the settings ("Hide Non-Video Participantso"), so that only participants with the camera switched on are visible. This creates a stage-like situation in which, for example, two or more players improvise, play a scene with each other or play a role-playing game. The actors are visible, but not the spectators; however, the spectators remain audible when needed.

Apart from Zoom and the digital pinboard "Padlet" (www.padlet.com), I rarely use other online tools. The idea is that in my workshop, interaction always comes first and the technology should remain in the background.

Interaction – camera and microphone on

In order to be able to work really interactively, small groups are needed. That is why I work online with a maximum of 14 participants and focus on the lively activity together, the constant exchange with the participants or animated dialogue between them.

Times must also be adjusted, as online teaching is actually demanding and quite exhausting. Ideal are blocks of a maximum of 3 1/2 hours per day (including 30-minute break). Daily units of 90 minutes distributed over several days also works well. If there's no alternative, I will also work online for a whole day and plan longer breaks for this. In addition, it is important that the participants are alone in their rooms and cannot be disturbed.

A necessary prerequisite for effective online work is that the participants leave their camera switched on. In order to be in contact with all participants, I almost always switch on the gallery view. Even when I am presenting myself, I try to keep an eye on all participants as much as possible, see their reactions and receive immediate feedback on the process.

Contrary to all official advice, I *don't* look at the camera, but at the participants. Their immediate feedback is more important to me because I can straight away refer to a smile or a frown and ask, clarify, build on consent, etc. Through this contact, the participants feel addressed and seen. Ideally, however, the camera should be mounted in such a way that more or less a feeling of eye contact is created.

Also going against the current "received wisdom," I ask the participants to leave their microphones on most of the time. On the one hand, this allows them to get involved spontaneously, and on the other hand, the background sounds create a lively conversation space that is soothingly reminiscent of "normal" interaction situations: you can hear very real people laughing, breathing, sighing, harrumphing, etc. For me as a trainer, this feedback is important to get a sense of the dynamics and the process, that is, as monitoring information, so that real interactive and spontaneous collaboration can be created.

In order to avoid unnecessary background noise, I'll usually invite the participants to look for a quiet and undisturbed workplace for the workshop and to ensure that no other people are present in the room.

This also makes it easier for participants to ask questions, volunteer for exercises, express themselves and experiment. I therefore also invite them to speak up at any time, as in a face-to-face workshop, without raising their hands first. This sometimes leads to two people starting to speak simultaneously. Most of the time, this only lasts a moment – it's worth it for the spontaneous expression and vibrancy that can enter the virtual space.

A major disadvantage of online workshops is that the participants are relatively easily distracted and also answer their emails, for example. This is one reason why many people are so exhausted after an online day: multitasking is and remains very strenuous. This makes it all the more important that the participants can be active and feel involved or, to a certain extent, jointly responsible for the joint success. This is much easier in shorter time blocks and allows participants to concentrate and get involved better. People can be "activated" by, for example:

- questions
- addressing participants directly
- exercises and role-playing games
- breakout sessions

Chat

I leave the private chat function off because I know from my own experience how much attention is lost when chat messages are exchanged on the side. In general, I try to avoid side conversations and make the lessons as transparent as possible. To this end, chat messages are set so that they come to everyone or just to me as host.

If possible, I prefer questions to come directly to me, as I want to focus on the content, the process and, above all, the participants and their learning during the lesson.

In online seminars, I see from time to time that hosts use the chat feature to collect answers to questions or comments about the content. Then, the hosts read the posts aloud, and the participants don't have their say for quite a while. In some cases, this saves time and increases the hosts' control of the course, which can be quite useful in certain situations (just before the break). However, the position of the host then monopolises the proceedings and can be at the expense of dynamics and interactivity.

Participant versus host centring

Online teaching is often very focused on the host (the course manager), who takes up most of the speaking time and is the focus for most of the time. This form of teaching has again increased considerably in online teaching, so in many webinars, you can see the course manager in large format, with the participants – if visible at all – squeezed around the narrow margin. Interaction is obviously less welcome, and if it is, then only via chat.

As in my classroom seminars, in online lessons, I try to focus on the participants. For example, I only share PowerPoint slides very briefly or only for as long as necessary, in order to quickly restore direct contact. In addition, I work almost exclusively in the gallery view, in order to keep an eye on everyone as much as possible and to support a group feeling.

What we say ourselves sticks in our memory significantly better than what we merely hear. That is why I constantly involve the participants in my questions as well as my exercises and try to convey theoretical backgrounds in exactly the same way. This means that in most cases, I do not start with a theory, but with a concrete experience in the form of an exercise, as an example. Only then do I evaluate the exercise together with the participants by asking questions and develop the theory in dialogue with them. Only at the very end, more or less as a summary, do I share my PowerPoint slides on the theory. At the end of the workshop, I place my slides in the chat to serve as a reminder afterwards.

After a workshop, it should be clear why the lessons had to take place live, rather than simply being recorded, to be viewed by the participants at any time. That's why I use the term "online workshop," not "webinar."

Script

Trainers in some circles refer to lesson planning as "seminar design." I like this term very much because it also includes the artistic aspect of good workshop planning. In online lessons today, one often speaks of a "script," and, as with a script for a film, there are indeed a lot of details to set down.

Here is an example of a script from one of my online workshops:

Time	Exercise	Form of work	Comments	Gathering suggestions
9:30–9:40	I'm a Tree	Plenary (all participants)		
9:40–9:50	No – yes, but ... – yes, and ...	Partner work in breakout sessions	Three rounds of three minutes. First, in plenary, briefly demonstrate the exercises with someone.	Once per round
9:50–10:00	Evaluation of the exercise	Plenary	Evaluation questions: How did the three rounds develop? What do you hear most often in your everyday life? When is it important to accept offers?	
10:00–10:10	Hollywood Swing	Partner work in breakout sessions	First, in plenary, briefly demonstrate the exercises with someone.	

In improvisational theatre, suggestions are often drawn as inspiration from the audience. I also use this dynamic element in my workshops. For example, in the "No – yes, but . . . – yes, and . . . " exercise, each round requires an occasion or event is needed, which should be planned together. This can be a summer party in the department, a company anniversary, a Christmas party, etc.

If the quality of face-to-face workshops depends very much on a coherent inner process, for online events, this coherence is even more essential. For example, it's not possible to stand in a circle and take turns. Instead, it's necessary to define clearly in advance what order will be applied. Often I let the participants say the name of the next person and thus determine the order. Another option is to add numbers to the names of the participants to establish a clear order. In the future, I hope that there will be even more technical possibilities here. With Zoom, it is already possible to move the video windows, but unfortunately, this arrangement is not yet visible to everyone.

As in face-to-face workshops, I only explain online exercises after enough participants have volunteered. Thus, they have to take a step into the unknown, but at the same time, they are under less pressure to be especially "good."

Large groups

It's also possible to work interactively with large groups, but in a different form. For each unit of 90 minutes, I look for a group of six volunteers. These six participants turn their camera on, while all the others turn their camera off and select the video setting "Hide Non-Video Participants," so that only the six people from the active group are visible.

With the volunteers, I show the exercises, clarify questions and evaluate the exercises. All other participants can ask and answer questions in breakout sessions or in the chat. Normally, the questions from the active group are representative of the whole group. It makes sense to have someone on hand for technical backup.

After each break, I create a new group so that different people are visible. In the breakout sessions, of course, everyone has to turn their cameras on again and then switch them off again in the plenary, except for the six participants from the active group.

Experimenting online

The improvisational theatre scene started relatively quickly with its first online experiments and also set out to exploit the technical possibilities, for example, participating in a Zoom workshop via smartphone and thus being able to shift scenes to other rooms (the kitchen, the hallway, etc.). Or preparing two identical objects that then seem to be passed from video window to video window, etc. The desire to play, try out and improvise with the technical possibilities was and is always great.

An important step for me was to open up these possibilities for non-professional improv players, that is, for applied improvisation. The important questions were: Which exercises are possible online and which are not? What do non-improv players like to do online? What could scare them off? It was a question of exploring the limits of this specific online work. Another question was how exercises could not only be implemented technically but also be comprehensibly explained online, within a realistic timeframe. It became clear that a surprisingly large number of exercises are easily explainable and feasible online, while others are difficult or impossible to transfer to an online format.

At my first workshop with applied improvisation, I was surprised by people's very great willingness to engage in these exercises online. Perhaps, the spatial distance has even contributed to the lowering of some inhibition thresholds. However, if something doesn't go quite so smoothly, an exercise stalls, or doesn't work as planned, it's harder to shrug it off compared to a classroom workshop. This makes it all the more important that I have a good view of the participants and can read their verbal and non-verbal reactions and the overall mood.

This book is certainly just a start. In the next few years, the technical possibilities for online workshops are expected to increase rapidly. There will be a large number of teachers who will experiment with it and try new things. A lot will be possible online, while much will still work better in the classroom.

Pros and cons of face-to-face versus online workshops

Online workshops are very useful for training social skills, which can then be applied both in online collaboration and in the workplace, for example:

- accepting offers and being in the moment
- making team members look good
- taking the lead and letting ourselves be guided
- failing with good humour
- creating and using stories
- status behaviour and status flexibility

The experience of the last few months shows that with applied improvisation, interpersonal connection can be established and trust can be built online. However, there are also certain limits in this respect. For example, online workshops are unlikely to achieve the potential impact of face-to-face workshops when it comes to topics such as:

- team development (except in emergency situations, for example, in the event of a lockdown)
- management of conflicts and ethical issues
- innovation or co-creative work with the aim of developing a common product or a new solution
- work on mission statements, vision and strategy

When workshops on these topics take place online for purely economic reasons or for other savings, they are quickly shown to lack depth and credibility. Online workshops in this context are promising if the necessary skills for cooperation are to be trained and a face-to-face workshop is not possible or does not make sense for ecological reasons.

Conclusion for social online learning

- short units
- small groups
- do not put technology in the foreground
- work interactively, keeping the camera and microphones on
- precise planning and clear processes
- training of social skills online – yes; team developments online – no (or only in emergency situations)
- try, experiment and have fun
- and – as always applies – fail with good humour

Chapter 2

Creativity

2.1 Introduction to (co-)creativity

Our human ability to create something new leads us into the future, which we ourselves shape through acts of creativity. The idea of the lonely but ingenious inventor still haunts our minds in the form of myths of legendary innovations. It was almost always men whose creative output makes our lives easier today and whose names we learn in school. In the vast majority of cases, however, several people were involved in these inventions, inspiring, researching and collaborating in the work. But no one remembers their names and their contribution today. Every technical, scientific, even creative breakthrough builds upon existing experiences and existing knowledge. An essential achievement is to work in the mode of so-called "co-creativity," an ability that should not be underestimated, especially in this day and age, in view of the global, networked, highly complex problems of our world. These problems are of a magnitude hardly comprehensible or manageable by individuals – however, ingenious individual minds may be. They clearly require co-creative efforts and cooperation.

From a group dynamic point of view, the following elements are considered to be prerequisites for successful co-creativity:

1 A problem exists, whose solution is important to all the people involved.
2 A suitable solution is not yet in sight or there is no central person (expert, manager, project manager, etc.) who already knows and could deliver the solution.
3 The parties involved are dependent on each other in problem-solving and/or finding solutions and are aware of this.

DOI: 10.4324/9781003172765-2

For any kind of co-creative collaboration, it is as characteristic as it is fundamental that after the work has been done, the whole team receives the recognition it deserves. In scientific research, however, individual performance is still often in the foreground. Competition for resources and recognition often leads stakeholders to compete over who can put their name to the results published. The European Organization for Nuclear Research in western Switzerland leads by example, listing the names of all participants in alphabetical order, no matter how large or small their contribution is (Beglinger, 2013).

With all that said, it is certainly no surprise that co-creativity is regarded as the absolute basis of joint improvisation because improvisation, the inventing of stories in the moment, is common, co-creative innovation. The "What Comes Next" exercise, for example, is a perfect training facility: As with many exercises by Keith Johnstone, responsibility is laid upon several shoulders. On the one hand, cooperation is indispensable; on the other hand, the players on stage are less pressured – which benefits the individual and common creativity, the original, free, perhaps unusual expression outside of familiar patterns of thought and action.

For the "What Comes Next" exercise online, two volunteers are needed from among the participants. Then, all the other participants turn off their cameras and select "Hide Non-Video Participants," so that only the two players are still visible, but all the others are audible. What the players should do or say now is dictated to them by the listeners.

Such scenes often begin like this:

> Player A: *"What comes next?"*
> Person from the audience: *"You say: It's nice to see you here."*
> Player A: *"It's nice to see you here!"*
> Player B: *"What comes next?"*
> Person from the audience: *"You turn away and say: We don't know each other."*
> Player B turns away and says, *"We don't know each other."*

Here, as a workshop leader, I have to draw attention to the blockage and help the audience look for new ways to accept the first offer, for example:

> Player B: *"What comes next?"*
> Person from the audience: *"You say: I've been waiting for you here for hours. I have to tell you something."*
> Player B: *"I've been waiting for you here for hours. I have to tell you something."*

Player A: "*What comes next?*"
Person from the audience: "*You say: Do you want to tell me that you are in love with me?*"
Player A: "*Do you want to tell me that you are in love with me?*"
Player B: "*What comes next?*"
Person from the audience: "*You say: Yes, exactly, since the first class.*"
Player B: "*Yes, exactly, since the first class.*"
. . . and so on.

Now, the audience is working together and develops a story together. In this exercise, the players often block each other, don't build on each other's ideas and don't allow themselves to be influenced or changed by each other. Therefore, the main aim of the host is to point this out step by step and to address, support and promote co-creative cooperation.

Separating the generation and evaluation of ideas

In co-creative processes, it is not only helpful but also crucial to separate the generation of ideas from their evaluation. The true creative phase, the "journey through unknown territory," thrives on the fact that offers are made, accepted, expanded and further built upon. In this phase, free thinking, association, appropriate action, etc., are required, whereas evaluations – even positive ones – are out of place.

It is often difficult enough to accept our own ideas and to say them out loud. Especially, if they are unusual, oblique or absurd, or at least seem like they are. Here, it helps not to concentrate on coming up with our own "genius" ideas but to practise letting go of our own ideas and building on the ideas of others. In this way, something new can be jointly created more easily. However, so that ideas do not simply "take off" and become unrealistic, it is possible and sensible to set a framework here, for example, with regard to time and/or costs. Only then will the analysis and selection come and here, of course, it is also necessary to decide against proposals, and if necessary also to say "no."

In many areas, zero fault tolerance is vital, for example, in air traffic control, hospitals and the production of chemical substances. In the case of creative processes, however, it must be possible to make "mistakes" without constantly having serious and dangerous consequences in mind. When new things are developed, the outcome is always uncertain at first. That's why the separation of the generation and evaluation of ideas is so important.

Failing with good humour

Improvisational theatre even makes mistakes a virtue and propagates "failing with good humour" freely, according to the motto *"Mistakes are the portals of discovery"* from James Joyce. When improvising, this specific form of conscious imperfection succeeds if – and only if – mistakes are welcomed. This ability, which runs counter to our own learning and social norms, has great potential! Quite a few inventions have arisen from errors, for example, Post-its, which originated with the search for a super adhesive. The experiments went badly wrong because the adhesive could be detached far too easily. Years later, a man named Art Fry used this glue so that, in the church choir, the bookmarks no longer fell out of his hymnbooks: the Post-it was invented!

Vaccination, too, came about through a mistake. Louis Pasteur injected certain bacteria into his chickens, which most chickens did not survive. While on holiday, he interrupted the trials, leaving a bacterial sample unused. He administered these bacteria to the chickens on his return. All the chickens survived this procedure because the bacteria had been damaged by the heat and thus attenuated. When he later injected these and other chickens with fresh bacteria, the only birds to survive were those that had earlier received the attenuated dose.

In my workshops, I make mistakes again and again. Not only do I not try to gloss over them and hide them but also I am certain that the participants will definitely learn something from me, even if it's just not doing it the way I did. Which wouldn't be all that seldom. Recently, for example, I pretty much failed in an online role-playing game: I took over from a participant and tried to deal competently with a difficult conversation situation. At one point, I didn't know what to say any more and gave up. As we reflected on this, the participant in question said something very interesting: that she was very happy about this "failed" role-playing game, that it showed her that this is a really difficult situation and that she has not just been "stupid" so far. As in this example, I always try to address my mistakes and thus strengthen the basis for real joint learning.

In online training, difficulties are often to be expected. The technology doesn't work, one participant has already dropped out of the online classroom, another doesn't even get in, someone's internet connection is bad, the sound equally so, a child runs through the picture in the background, etc. As always, it is also a matter of keeping calm, solving the problems one after the other as far as possible and making the most of the situation, that is, saying "yes, and . . . " to creative chaos (Figure 2.1).

Figure 2.1 © Evi Fill

2.2   **Creativity online**

The corona pandemic has massively accelerated digital change in a very short time. Home office has become a genuine alternative to working on company premises, and further training takes place online. That these changes are establishing new standards is shown by the fact that quite a few companies are already reducing office space, or seminar providers are completely switching their training courses to webinars. This development seems to be just the beginning. When physical presence in the company is no longer imperative (or no longer seems to be), companies will carefully consider how to further reduce costs. And if home office is possible within the same city or country, it doesn't technically make any differences whether that home office is moved to another continent – with costs, worker protection and other legal obligations far below local conditions and standards.

Creative collaboration cannot so easily be moved into virtual space. In the future, significant innovations will continue to require direct social contact. And this can only be created in part through virtual cooperation: for example, occupational psychologist Oliver Strohm states, "*Direct exchange in trusting relationships accelerates innovation*" (quoted from Mordrelle, 2020). Face-to-face contact, therefore, remains indispensable to creativity and innovation for the "invention of the future."

On the basis of established contact and reasonable trust, co-creativity can be trained very well online and with methods from improvisational theatre! This applies in particular to the following skills:

- practising association, as a direct path to the unconscious
- dismantling our own blockages to creativity
- developing ideas and letting them go
- taking up offers and building on them
- . . . and so on

2.3 Phases of the creative process

Joy Paul Guilford coined the concept of "divergent thinking" and described the process of just how new ideas are created by the participants dealing with a topic openly and experimentally. While (supplementary and not contradictory!) *convergent* thinking is about linear, logical, rational ways of thinking in the context of problem-solving, *divergent* thinking is deliberately designed to eliminate critical objections, as they limit intellectual room for manoeuvre and thus reduce the variety of possible solutions. Here, even solutions that cannot be implemented at first are seen as possible and even necessary, as they can lead to a better understanding of the problem and ultimately to new, unconventional solutions.

In creative processes, it is ideally divergent thinking that prevails! On the one hand, however, associations and changes of perspective are necessary for this. And on the other hand, a conscious sequence and discipline with regard to the process steps: only *after* the creativity phase should evaluation and selection take place, however great the pressure for success or as tempting as the desire for quick, tangible solutions is.

Basically, each creative process goes through several phases:

1   *Analysis.* First of all, the problem must be analysed: what is the purpose of finding a new solution in the first place? What is the goal? Do the parties involved have a common objective?
2   *Brainstorming.* Only when the problem is sufficiently known and recognised as such can the generation of ideas be started. Here, all techniques from the improvisational theatre come into play, for example, postponing criticism and instead saying "yes, and . . .," to allow associations, to welcome the unconscious and to let go of one's own ideas again.
3   *Evaluation and selection.* In this phase, the proposed solutions are systematically evaluated, and the most promising solution is developed.
4   *Implementation.* The implementation of a solution almost inevitably creates new problems, for which new solutions must be found in turn. So, the process is circular and thus starts again from the beginning, with analysis.

2.4   Creativity and agility

Until not so long ago, in German-speaking countries, the word "agility" described the well-preserved physical and mental agility of mainly older people. In the last decades of the 20th century, the term then experienced a whole new lease of life. Companies oriented towards stability and security were "suddenly" confronted with rapid changes, great complexity and a great deal of uncertainty. In this context, agility quickly gained popularity and was for a while considered a universal requirement for success: being agile now meant the paradigm of being able to predict changes and reacting faster and more flexibly to them. In other words, no longer excluding uncertainty and insecurity as undesirable disruptive factors, but on the contrary, welcoming them and learning to operate proactively. Digital transformation made its contribution to these changes in attitude.

Agility refers, on the one hand, to methods and tools ("doing agile"). But this is based upon values and principles ("being agile"). An agile approach therefore includes not only organisational processes but also successful cooperation and communication in companies. Ideally, agile

organisations are characterised by transparency, dialogue, trust, participation and short-term feedback mechanisms.

A classic agile method is "Scrum." Scrum originates from software
technology and is now used in many areas. Scrum relies on interdisci-
plinary development teams that are set a target and are responsible for
the implementation themselves. They are therefore non-hierarchic and
well suited to solving complex problems. This self-management allows
the knowledge and creativity of the teams concerned to fully develop
and achieve greatest impact.

Agility and improvisation

The origin of all agile methods is that long-term developments were
becoming more and more unpredictable and, instead of being planned
meticulously, often had to be handled spontaneously, and changes had to
be faced through improving together. Critical to success is not so much
the sophisticated methodical "hardware" but ultimately people's awareness of the potential of interaction.

Improvisational theatre offers an excellent opportunity to profit from
existing potential and to convey and build attitudes and approaches by
having fun. Changes are structurally creative processes! Agility and
improvisational ability are qualities that can be trained like a muscle.
Well-trained, they also enable us to respond appropriately to situations of
uncertainty and to manage changes in a forward-looking manner.

The Scrum method defined five values for how agile teams work together.
These have many parallels in the basics of co-creative improvisation:

1 Commitment

The team is guided by its goals, is ready to fully engage and takes responsibility for the work.

In improv theatre, too, it is necessary to commit ourselves fully to
the common purpose! Admittedly, this is not always easy, for example,
when a scene on stage goes wrong and the audience seems bored. How
much easier it would be to stay on the edge of the scene and not support
our teammates! Every story on stage is co-creative at its core. That's
why everyone is always involved and therefore responsible for making
things go well on stage – but also for making them go badly. Here, the
only thing that helps is to fully engage in cooperation, to vow an inner
"in good times as well as in bad times," as it were. Whether on stage or
in a company.

Commitment means not only having good ideas of our own and enforcing them but also letting go of our own ideas. This virtue can be practised very well with the "One-sentence Story" exercise. Online, each player is given a number. Then, in order, a joint story is told, with each player being allowed to contribute only one sentence. It is impossible to plan ahead because the story is constantly changing. Participants must therefore consistently let go of their own ideas in favour of the joint story. Commitment therefore also means putting the success of the team before our own success. Of course, the team must also be rewarded in the end and not the individual performance.

2   Focus

Distraction also costs a lot of money and time in companies. For this reason, agile cooperation attaches great importance to applying the necessary concentration and focus. Interruptions, disturbances and misunderstandings are therefore eliminated as soon as possible.

In improvisation, we practise alert listening and attention in the here and now. It is crucial to receive and accept the offers of our fellow players because these are the source of our own inspiration. In addition, as improv players, we have to note and remember as much as possible: the suggestions from the audience, for example, the names of the other characters on stage or the objects that our partners have introduced to the stage through pantomime, etc. All these are only possible if concentration and attention are kept at a constantly high level.

This ability can be trained online, for example, with the "Birthday Messages" exercise. Here, the participants (five to six volunteers) send birthday video greetings to a fictional person whose birthday it is. This is defined more precisely by each greeting (How old is the person? What does the do they like? In what relationships do they live? etc.). Only those who listen closely to the other messages can then refer to them. In the end, the person with the birthday (another volunteer) thanks the people sending greetings and refers to the messages and their (co-)created identity.

3   Openness

Openness and transparency are among the most important values of agile cooperation. In the procedures described, from problem analysis to the realisation of implementation steps, not only communication must flow as freely and unhindered as possible: ideas, assumptions and criticism, but also errors and suggestions for improvement must be addressed directly. The quality of the cooperation (who has how much influence, attention, speaking time, trust, etc.) must also be addressed with the help of metacommunication.

In certain places, a "no" is just as important in team and creativity processes as the "yes, and . . . ". It stands for a crucial difference (of opinion) and for the indispensable courage needed to oppose a group majority or authority. The relevant literature reports on countless disasters that would have been avoided if co-pilots had been able to prevail against captains, engineers against space mission commanders, etc. Withstanding even great pressure is a personal ability, and like every personality trait is determined by multiple factors.

In terms of deepening and further developing this ability, classical (i.e. beyond individual experience) group dynamics training has proven to be highly effective. Especially, in self-organised teams, in which not everything is managed and determined by a leader, there must inevitably be more conflicts. It is no coincidence that "those who do not fight have already lost." The aim of this type of necessary conflict is to achieve the best possible result, a synthesis of legitimate and conflicting interests, through the dispute and a fair negotiation process. The fact that mature, stable players and non-opportunistic yes-sayers are needed here means that well-developed and anchored basic group dynamic skills are all the more important, especially in agile teams.

In both improvisation and creative team processes, the "Yes, and . . . " stands for listening to and respecting other opinions. In a conflict, it can simply read: "Yes, and I accept that you disagree." In addition, it means saying "yes, and . . . " to both one's own impulses and those of the other person. By taking up ideas and adopting them as a common basis, new things are created together. This kind of openness can best be trained with the diverse methods of improvising and is a wonderful "fuel" for continuous production of ideas.

A suitable exercise online is "Hollywood Swing": two players go together into a breakout session and invent the plot of a film together by always answering with "*Yes exactly, and.*" A player starts and says, for example:

Player A: "*You made this great movie, which is about a start-up.*"
Player B: "*Yes exactly, and . . . at first these two women are grappling with their fate as single mothers.*"
Player A: "*Yes exactly, and . . . then they have the idea of connecting with other single mothers.*"
Player B: "*Yes exactly, and . . . then they set up this online network for single mothers who support each other.*"

Player A: "*Yes exactly, and . . . with that they become so successful that in the end one of them runs for president.*"

Player B: "*Yes exactly, and . . . in the end she wins and actually becomes the first female president of the United States.*"

For agile teams, the separate handling of openness to ideas and the evaluation of ideas is particularly helpful. Any proposal can have the potential to offer a surprising, new, unusual solution if everyone does their part.

4 Respect

Respect is another important value of Scrum. And although fundamental to any successful interpersonal coexistence, respect is quickly lost under pressure. It is similar to many rules of engagement that can be found on every poster on communication guidelines in the team or seminar room. Astonishingly, often, the same rules are there, for example:

* We let each other talk.
* We treat each other with respect.
* We are tolerant.
* . . . and so on.

These rules of conduct are easy to implement when everything is going well. And are often thrown overboard at the first sign of difficulty.

Improv theatre, however, has the following rule: "Let others look good." This maxim cleverly directs the focus away from oneself to one's opposite number – and would also be good for friendly relations, including couples! For example, what if a fellow player is on stage, about to start a scene, but suddenly has a blackout? Well, another player could step in and take over the scene. Alternatively, they could come in and say: "*Is this your first job interview too? I'm so nervous!*" In which scene does the first player look better? Right!

The Canadian improv duo "Crumbs" has developed a format called "Your 15 Minutes of Fame." In the process, a random member of the audience is brought onto the stage, and the two improv players integrate them so skilfully into their scene that the impression is given that the spectator is an experienced improv player. This can only be achieved if the players make the newcomer look good every minute.

The exercise "Giving Gifts" also helps to train this ability. The exercise is performed in pairs in breakout sessions. One player presents a gift to the other and says what it is, for example.

Player A: *"I brought you a gift. It's a key to your new house."*
Player B accepts the gift and replies: *"Thank you, I've wanted space for my own workshop for so long!"*

Then the players swap roles:

Player B: *"I brought you a gift. It's a voucher for a weekend with your best friend."*
Player A: *"Thank you! I've been wanting to go to a spa with my girlfriend for so long!"*

The task of the players is to give each other something that makes the other look good and at the same time brings them joy. For this, it is necessary to be attentive and to put oneself in the other's shoes. Even if the players don't know each other yet or not very well.

5   Courage

Self-organisation can lead to a loss of orientation and thus insecurity or a certain instability. Enduring emerging insecurity, dealing with conflicts constructively and taking responsibility for one's own actions require not a little courage to dare to take steps into the unknown or to dare to trust oneself and others "on unstable ground."

Improvisational theatre demands and supports courage: as a player, you stand on stage and have nothing. No text, no props and no costume. You have to rely on yourself and your teammates. The real art of improvisation is to remain calm and be able to act in moments of great uncertainty and high pressure. No wonder, this outstanding resource is also in demand in agile teams!

But courage is also needed to admit or address mistakes. In agile teams, learning from mistakes is essential. To do this, however, mistakes must first be disclosed and not covered up!

Kelly Leonard and Tom Yorton are members of the group The Second City, the most successful comedy stage and improvisation school in the United States. In their book "Yes and – Lessons from The Second City" (Leonard & Yorton, 2015), they provide valuable tips on how best to fail:

1   Fail publicly: don't hide mistakes
2   Fail together: with real teamwork, it is never just an individual's fault
3   Fail without judgement: do not look for someone to blame
4   Fail with confidence: believe in the potential of mistakes
5   Fail gradually: detect as early as possible when mistakes happen

These five points are an excellent guide to dealing with mistakes in self-directed teams.

The courage to fail with good humour, to handle pressure playfully and to be able to act in unforeseen situations can also be very well trained with PowerPoint Karaoke (see p. 76).

Conclusion

Improvisational theatre is geared towards collaboration and creativity; companies towards agility and innovation. In contrast to Scrum, for example, improvisational theatre is not a method that can be implemented directly in companies, leading directly to tangible innovations. Improvisational theatre, however, can very well and successfully lay the foundations of co-creative cooperation in companies, on which further agile resources can be developed! Improvisational theatre strengthens cohesion and relationships, trains attention, improves interpersonal and professional communication and nurtures creativity and flexibility. All these skills are essential for agile collaboration.

2.5 Exercises for creativity online

As already stated, creativity and co-creative processes can be trained very well online. Not everything, however, can be moved into virtual space at will. That's why I recommend combining online work with face-to-face meetings whenever possible and taking advantage of both forms.

In this chapter, I describe some exercises that have proven themselves very well online.

The "Yes, and . . . " principle – accept offers

First of all, it is about the basic understanding of "accepting offers" and experiencing the potential effect of this openness first hand.

Exercise

Online "No – yes, but . . . – yes, and . . . "

This exercise is done in pairs in three rounds. First, with a partner, demonstrate the task of the first round and then send the pairs to breakout sessions for a few minutes. Then, bring them back and show the task of the second round with another partner. Each round has an event to be planned, and this event is proposed by someone from the group.

FIRST ROUND

Question to the group: "*What event would you like to plan?*" Participant proposal: "*A company's Christmas party.*"

A player then makes an offer to another to plan this event and that player has to answer "no" to it and then make an alternative offer:

> Player A: "*Let's have the Christmas party on a ship.*"
> Player B: "*No, that's far too expensive – best we celebrate here in the company.*"
> Player A: "*No, that's way too boring – let's invite a cool band.*"
> . . . and so on.

SECOND ROUND

For example, a participant suggests a "*birthday party*" as an event.

This time, the players always answer with "Yes, but . . . " and then make an offer themselves:

> Player A: "*Let's just invite my family.*"
> Player B: "*Yes, but they always fight. Let's have the party in my garden.*"
> Player A: "*Yes, but then the whole garden will be ruined. Let's celebrate in a restaurant.*"
> . . . and so on.

THIRD ROUND

One player makes an offer, and the other player has to respond with a "Yes, and . . .," and their follow-up offer. This time, a "*divorce*" is planned:

> Player A: "*Let's celebrate our divorce with a big party.*"
> Player B: "*Yes, and we invite everyone who has stood by us during our marriage.*"

Player A: *"Yes, and we drink a lot of alcohol."*
Player B: *"Yes, and we forgive each other all our affairs."*
Player A: *"Yes, and at the end we fall into each other's arms."*
Player B: *"Yes, and then we make a marriage proposal to each other."*

. . . and so on.

TECHNOLOGY

- Breakout sessions: partner work in three rounds

For evaluation, I ask the pairs the following questions:

- How did these three rounds feel and what changed between them?
- What do you hear most often in your life (no, yes or yes, and)?
- When do you need the "yes, and . . . " in your working life? (e.g. teamwork, co-creativity, collaboration and motivation of colleagues)

The following exercises are then useful to better identify when offers are being blocked or accepted:

Exercise

Online "Hollywood Swing"

This exercise is performed in pairs, in breakout sessions. First, demonstrate the exercise with a partner. One of them is a director and has made a film – the other has seen the film. That one starts and says:

Player A: *"You made such a great film, all about ants."* (Doesn't matter what!)
From now on, all the answers must start with "Yes, exactly, and."
Player B: *"Yes, exactly, and these ants climb up all the houses."*
Player A: *"Yes, exactly, and then they eat their way through the walls."*
Player B: *"Yes exactly, and people have to flee from the ants."*

. . . and so on.

Together, the pair comes up with a film plot, and no one knows beforehand where it will lead. What is important is not to recount the making-of, but the plot of the film. In summary, the two players give their newly storyboarded masterpiece a suitable title – again invented then and there! It is precisely this summary and conclusion that frequently causes a lot of hilarity due to the often very funny and sometimes quirky titles.

TECHNOLOGY

- Breakout sessions: partner work

Exercise

Online "Who Can Block Offers Better?"

First, two volunteers are needed. The two players begin to improvise an everyday scene together (e.g. two colleagues in an online meeting). Their job is to block all offers. If a player accepts an offer, they are replaced. One of those watching then turns on their camera and jumps in for the player who accepted the offer, and the scene continues from where it was interrupted – until the next offer is accidentally accepted.

Being allowed to block is usually a lot of fun for the participants. At the same time, it raises awareness of what a block is and why it leads stories to a dead end.

Online "Who Can Accept Offers Better?"

This exercise is the same, except that this time all offers have to be accepted. It's great for training.

TECHNOLOGY

- All viewers turn off their cameras so that only the players are visible. To do this, all participants must select "Hide Non-Video Participants" in their video settings.

Exercise

Online "What Comes Next?"

All participants, with the exception of two volunteers, turn off their camera. One of the volunteers starts and asks, *"What comes next?"* A spectator spontaneously offers an instruction as to what to do and/or say. Then, the volunteer does/says that, after which the other player continues with *"What's next?"*, etc. The players just do and say what the audience tells them to do. It is important to build on the existing offers, so the audience and the players work together in a co-creative way!

> Player A begins with the question: *"What comes next?"*
> Someone in the audience says, *"You say, 'Lovely to see you here, Dr Maier!'"*
> Player A: *"Lovely to see you here, Dr Maier!"*
> Player B: *"What comes next?"*
> Someone from the audience says, *"Likewise, likewise, Professor Müller. Your presentation earlier was quite excellent!"*
> Player B: *"Likewise, likewise, Professor Müller. Your presentation earlier was quite excellent!"*
> Player A: *"What comes next?"*
> Someone from the audience says: *"Thank you, these online conferences, they're still unfamiliar! So you are also dealing with the changes in the digital world. Would you be interested in cooperating in the future?"*
> Player A: *"Thank you, these online conferences, they're still unfamiliar! So you are also dealing with the changes in the digital world. Would you be interested in cooperating in the future?"*
> Player B: *"What comes next?"*
> Someone in the audience says, *"I'd love to!"*
> Player B: *"I'd love to!"*

> . . . and so on.

TECHNOLOGY

• All spectators turn off their cameras so that only the two players are visible. To do this, all participants must select "Hide Non-Video Participants" in their video settings.

Exercise

Online "Giving Gifts"

First, demonstrate this exercise with a participant and then send all participants into breakout sessions in pairs to let them try the exercise for themselves. The first player presents a gift to the other and says:

> Player A: *"I brought you a gift – it's a long journey."*
> Player B accepts the gift and replies: *"Thank you very much! For a long time I've wanted to cycle to southern Italy."*
> Player A tries to find a gift that their teammate could really be happy about. Player B defines exactly what they do with the gift.

VARIANT

The first player mimes holding an object and tries to show the size and weight with their hands. Then, they hand over this imaginary object to their teammate and say, *"I brought you a gift!"* The recipient tries to take over the object in size and weight, then unpacks the gift and says, *"Oh thank you, a . . . (e.g. an elephant, a wedding ring, etc.)."*

TECHNOLOGY

- Breakout sessions: partner work

Associations

Creativity comes largely from the unconscious. That is why free access to this inexhaustible resource is so helpful. The more we censure ourselves (*"I'm not funny," "I have no ideas," "I'm embarrassed, lacking originality,"* etc.), the less the ideas bubble up out of us. Good improvisors can be so fascinating because they always have an answer, always a new idea.

When associating, conscious and unconscious thoughts are linked together, enabling a more effortless flow of thoughts. For example, this can be practised as follows:

Exercise

Online "Associations"

A player starts by saying a word and another player's name. That player must say the first word – that is, the first association – that comes to mind and then the name of the participant who is to continue.

VARIANT

One variation is that a player has to say as many associations as possible to a word in one minute. The difficulty can be increased by allowing only nouns or only verbs.

The next exercise is also about thinking associatively as quickly as possible:

Exercise

Online "Genre Object"

All participants take a pen in their hands. The moderator asks for a "genre." A volunteer starts by holding the pen to the camera, and saying what this pen now is in this genre, and calls the next name. The next participant then continues until everyone has had a go. Then, a new genre is defined.

For example, the first genre could be a romantic film:

> Player A holds up the pen and says, "*This is the English coastal landscape, and Andreas continues.*"
> Player B holds up the pen and says, "*This is the noble bachelor, and Martina continues.*"
> Player C holds up the pen and says, "*This is the fire in the hearth, and . . . continues.*"

This exercise is also suitable for teaching foreign languages or for repeating certain terms on a subject.

The next exercise is well suited for starting a workshop or after a break and also trains the ability to associate:

Exercise

Online "I feel ... like a ... "

A participant starts and says how he or she is feeling right now and compares it to something, for example:

> Player A: "*I feel tired, like a dried-up flower.*"
> Player B: "*I feel curious, like a cat.*"

Visual thinking

Strengthened visual thinking also increases creativity. For example, using the following exercise:

Exercise

Online "I Am a Tree"

A player starts by saying, for example, "*I'm a drone*" and tries to represent this with their hands. When the players try to physically represent their character/object in this small visual space, it becomes more fun, and it is also clearer to see who is playing and who is just watching. A second player then comes in and says, for example, "*I'm a YouTuber*" and again tries to portray it physically. Then, a third player comes along and says, for example, "*I'm the many clicks.*"

Then, the first player takes someone with them and says, for example, "*I'll take the YouTuber with me,*" or "*I take the many clicks with me.*" Both players then go back into a neutral position. The remaining player now repeats what they are, for example, "*I'm a YouTuber.*" Now, two players are added one after the other, and a new picture is created, and so on.

VARIANT

This exercise can also be played with cameras turned off, so that only the active players keep their cameras on.

Exercise

Online "Birthday Messages"

This exercise requires six volunteers. One after the other, the first five players send a short birthday video message to a fictional person whose birthday it is. At the beginning, the only information given is the person's name. Through the various birthday greetings, it is gradually defined who the person is. To do this, it is important to listen to others and build on each other. It helps if the players pretend to have a certain relationship with the person (the mother, the father, siblings, friends, etc.).

In the end, the sixth player takes on the role of the person with the birthday and thanks the others who have sent messages. In doing so, this player must also bear in mind and respond to the previous videos.

TECHNOLOGY

- All spectators turn off their cameras so that only the six players are visible. To do this, all participants must select "Hide Non-Video Participants" in their video settings.

Exercise

Online "New Choice"

This exercise is demonstrated first and then performed in breakout sessions. Two players talk about something (fictional) they have experienced together: for example, a holiday. The third player watches and can say "*new choice*" at any time, at which point the respective player has to come up with something else. This can also be said several times in a row, which makes this exercise more difficult, with less and less control and censorship over what is said.

> Player A: "*We were in Italy last summer. I liked it best when had ice cream together.*"
> Viewer: "*New choice.*"
> Player A: "*. . . when we went swimming together in the sea.*"
> Viewer: "*New choice.*"
> Player A: "*. . . when we jumped off the cliffs together.*"
> Player B: "*Yes, exactly, and then we went back to the hotel.*"
> Viewer: "*New choice.*"
> Player B: "*. . . and then we built that huge sandcastle.*"
> Etc.

TECHNOLOGY

- Breakout sessions: partner work

Chapter 3

Teamwork

3.1 Introduction to teamwork

Not everything that is called teamwork in everyday life is real teamwork. There is a small but crucial difference between a working group and people working in team mode. As long as the manager makes decisions autonomously, it is not real teamwork, but a working group, centrally controlled and only cooperating "serially." This is by no means a criticism against this form of work. A major advantage is that decisions can be made promptly if necessary and existing solutions or a proven path can be pursued without a lot of back and forth. If things have to be done quickly, such as in emergencies or other crisis situations, working groups have their advantages. One of these, of course, is the hierarchical structure, which legitimises decisions without distinct discussion processes if necessary.

Complex problems, however, call for co-creativity to first "invent" the future; then, real teamwork is required. Real teamwork puts more strain on the nerves, and experience shows it takes longer. For this, the rewards are higher quality and better acceptance among participants and stakeholders. In addition, the potential of the team members flows in, often only gradually unfolding in the process of overcoming the challenges. Decisions are made together and team members inspire, correct, contradict and encourage each other. Diversity is key! When team members have different backgrounds, complex relationships are viewed from different perspectives – broader, deeper, more diverse, etc. – in short, more appropriately. Mutual inspiration and planting of ideas included.

Cooperation in everyday professional life thrives on a successful combination of both forms of work and their different potentials and synergies. The exercises described later will be about inspiring and supporting real teamwork (Figure 3.1).

DOI: 10.4324/9781003172765-3

Figure 3.1 © Evi Fill

Psychological security

A while back, Google set about looking for success criteria for teams (Duhigg, 2016) and came to the conclusion that getting the best minds together in a team is actually not so important. The following factors have been identified as truly decisive:

- The team members must feel safe and comfortable in the team and be able to talk openly.
- The trust between the team members must be palpable.
- The speaking time is fairly evenly distributed between the team members.

Psychologist and engineer Amy Edmondson (2013) lists the following prerequisites for effective teamwork:

- Effective teamwork arises when everyone is open and interested in the needs, skills, interests and goals of the others, regardless of their hierarchical position.
- The aim of any teamwork is to integrate these different perspectives and thus to arrive at new solutions.
- To do this, participants need both affective (feeling) and cognitive (thinking) abilities.
- Paradoxes must be endured in the team and in the company, for example: play versus discipline, high standards versus error culture and specialists versus generalists.
- It is necessary to discover and address errors early in order to learn from them.

These prerequisites are covered by the term "psychological safety," coined by Amy Edmondson (2013), whereby the following key points are defined:

- Everyone can openly express their opinion.
- Questions may be asked.
- Mistakes are addressed and not punished.
- At the right time, doubt must be permitted.
- Dissenting opinions, differences, problems and conflicts are discussed.

Psychological safety is the basis for real teamwork or co-creative work in a team, and applied improvisation can serve very well to build it in teams!

In improvisational theatre, stories are invented jointly, in the "here and now," whereby there is no script and no director, meaning there is no clear hierarchy. Precisely because of this need for self-organisation, there arises real cooperation between the players. This co-creative collaboration requires a certain amount of training, no question. But fortunately, improv theatre provides many exciting exercises.

The "Yes, and . . . " principle in teams

As already described, co-creativity can only arise if proposals are accepted and jointly built upon. Confidence can also only arise if a person feels sure that their own opinion and ideas are heard, are taken up and are further developed.

Take the lead and let yourself be led

With real teamwork, all team members must be able to take the lead, but they must also be able to give up leadership and be guided. It is important that the focus is not on the ego of the parties involved, but on the common project.

Applied improvisation in teamwork

With the methods of applied improvisation, the following prerequisites for real teamwork are trained:

- Acknowledging and accepting offers
- Trying new things and opening up
- Building trust by getting to know new sides of each other
- Taking the lead and letting ourselves be guided
- Making mistakes and laughing about it

3.2 Teamwork online

If teamwork has to take place exclusively online, as for example in the case of a lockdown, this also has disadvantages to go along with all the hoped-for advantages. Online work costs energy and often motivation. Quite a few people find it hard to cope with many videoconferences, and they get tired or exhausted. No surprise that a term has been found for it: "Zoom fatigue."

Those informal conversations during the break, over coffee or in the corridor cannot take place. There is little exchange about personal or private things – except perhaps when the children storm the home office yet again. But mainly, emotions tend to fall by the wayside. In many online meetings, the approach is to get through the agenda as quickly as possible. It is often unclear whether everyone really needs to be present, and on top of this, presence has become even more volatile than in normal office conditions. Some don't appear at all for online meetings or have to leave again immediately. Others are there, but have turned off their camera. And others are apparently there, but continue to work on the side. After the meeting, everyone is on their own again, and as a result, many enriching encounters are eliminated, which would normally have created benefits on the side for the company.

In this context, first of all, it is important that online meetings should only take place when they are really necessary. This means that the information cannot be conveyed by other means and that everyone really needs to take part. But if these conditions do apply, then such meetings also need a high level of commitment! As far as possible, participation should be considered obligatory, all cameras and most microphones are switched on, and no other work is done on the side. But this can only be expected and demanded with a clear conscience, if the presence of each individual really matters (see real teamwork)!

The good news is that it is possible to create a genuine sense of belonging online and to deepen trust. This is the basis of any good teamwork and expresses itself, for example, in individuals' certainty that the other team members are working for the benefit of all and thus also for each individual and that they openly express their opinion, pass on important information and do their best. This strengthens motivation, personal connections and positive experiences in mutual interaction.

The following points help to create a climate of trust and commonality even in online meetings:

I   Allow time for personal and informal chat

It is helpful to start an online meeting with a short check-in, in which everyone can briefly share something personal about themselves (e.g. How am I doing today? How's the work going in general? What am I looking forward to? How are the children in homeschooling?). This means allowing space for the interpersonal and interest in the other participants when working at a distance. A short personal check-out at the end usually rounds off a meeting well.

Since informal exchanges are not so easy online, spaces can be created for them. This means, for example, that during work, some time is also reserved for personal, joint and interpersonal matters by celebrating something with each other online, for example, by raising a glass together. Or if everyone is working individually, they can still remain connected via videoconference and are thus able to talk and ask questions on the side. If you need a rest, just turn off the sound!

2 Explicit instead of implicit

It is often difficult to say openly and directly what we are thinking. Especially, if we disagree. Often, we express rejection and irritation only through our body language. Online, this is even harder because it is barely recognisable to others. So, it is all the more important online to express opinions clearly and openly. This means saying if we don't agree with something, even if we're the only one who doesn't. Or addressing the issue directly if another team member annoys us with their behaviour (e.g. doesn't let others finish speaking, is too domineering, or doesn't get involved at all). This may well mean additional irritation at first. But if this situation is managed well together, confidence will be created. Because we now know that our counterpart is not talking about us behind our back, but is telling us directly what is going on – this kind of adult interaction connects and provides security because we know that the other person thinks the relationship with us is important, even if it becomes difficult.

Openness towards hierarchical or professional superiors is also often not easy. Nevertheless, for real teamwork, there is no way around it. Openness must also be shown to those at management level and thus, for example, the new change project must be not only commented on or criticised informally, "round the houses" but also addressed or criticised directly. Then, the manager has a fair chance, but also the responsibility, to deal with it constructively.

3 Show and acknowledge emotions

Emotions are even less visible and harder to express online, but they're so fundamental to cooperation. Positive emotions trigger motivation, while negative emotions can connect, when they have space and are allowed to be there. Here, everyone can lead by example and address their own emotions. Negative feelings are often a signal that something is wrong in cooperation. This can at first also be expressed very vaguely, for example, in the form of listlessness, or an advanced stage of debilitating fatigue. If this lack of energy is new, it's often a sign of a blockage in teamwork. Then, it is time to address this and ask if others are feeling the same.

Positive emotions can arise through humour or through pleasant shared experiences. For example, in a team session, having the courage to try a loosening-up exercise (e.g. "Whac-A-Mole") or even to dance with each other (e.g. "Follow the Leader"). Personal stories (see chapter "Storytelling") are also a way to bring valuable emotions into everyday life online.

4   Have a clear structure and make clear decisions

Online meetings should preferably take place in small groups, otherwise interactive working is hardly possible. The working hours, goals and agenda of the meeting must be fixed beforehand, but still leave room for spontaneity. The session should be as compact as possible and allow enough breaks. In addition to short presentations and discussions, it is also important to integrate creative exercises and a lot of interaction (e.g. through breakout sessions). Having to listen to others for a long time and not being able to participate actively is much more strenuous and tiring online than in face-to-face meetings. The more interaction and participation the better!

It is also important to determine what decisions should be taken, who is involved and how those decisions are taken.

Constructive online meetings

Keith Johnstone, founder of the competitive improv form Theatresports, (Johnstone, 1998), formulated principles on how stories can be destroyed quickly and effectively. Applied to collaboration, *not* complying (!) with the so-called "destruction rules" supports productive and lively exchange in online team meetings:

Destruction rule 1: Block

> High jump coach A: "*Let's try out what happens when our athletes jump backwards over the pole.*"
> High jump coach B: "*Yes, but we've always jumped forwards and everyone else does that too.*"

Online, it is very demanding to listen to each other and take up offers. If you succeed in this, however, it is all the more motivating, and a feeling of cohesion can also arise online.

Conclusion for teamwork: Listen to, record and develop offers (e.g. Coach B: "*That's a wild idea that I'll try out for myself tomorrow in training!*")

Destruction rule 2: Apparent consent

> High jump coach A: "*Let's try out what happens when our athletes jump backwards over the pole.*"
> High jump coach B (grumpily): "*We could do that . . . .*"

Approval is only apparent; the idea has not really been taken up and developed. Implicit rejection is hardly recognisable online and certainly not approval *appears* to have been given.

Conclusion for teamwork: Explicitly address wishes, expectations, rejections and other opinions (e.g. Coach B: "*I think it's great that you keep coming up with new suggestions! We tried it once last year and our most important athlete got injured, so I don't want to try again.*")

Destruction rule 3: Be negative

> High jump coach A: "*Let's try out what happens when our athletes jump backwards over the pole.*"
> High jump coach B: "*Imagine what could happen! Think about the risk of injury and the fact that we could be excluded from competitions. The risk is far too high.*"

It is difficult for people to engage in change, especially if they have not chosen it themselves. It is very easy to block changes with a permanently negative attitude.

Conclusion for teamwork: Engage in change, but also take fears seriously, ask questions and search for solutions together (e.g. Coach A: "*I see that this proposal scares you. Tell you what, I'm just going to try it myself.*" Or when someone complains about videoconferencing: "*What exactly do you not like about videoconferencing? What should we do about it?*").

Destruction rule 4: Duck out

Compared to face-to-face events, online events are even easier terrain for freeloaders: they stay in the background, deactivate their camera, do not speak up and do not drive the action forward. In brief, they add little of value.

Conclusion for teamwork: Taking responsibility and helping to shape the proceedings.

Destruction rule 5: Dodge or distract

> High jump coach C: "*Should we try it now?*"
> High jump coach D: "*Yes, of course we can do that, but what I would like to discuss beforehand – and this is very important to me – it's that the new jerseys have just arrived, and . . .*"

There will never be a conclusion, which is all the more frustrating online.

Conclusion for teamwork: Take a position and make decisions, especially online (e.g. Person B: *"Yes, let's!"*)

Destruction rule 6: Gags

> High jump coach A: *"Let's try out what happens when our athletes jump backwards over the pole."*
>
> High jump coach B: *"Of course, you can also put the cart before the horse!"*

Some gags and jokes come at the expense of the common good and put the ego in the foreground. There is laughter, but the story and progress are halted.

Conclusion for teamwork: Place the ego in the background, focus on the common theme or goal – online and offline!

Destruction rule 7: Don't let others influence you

Keeping control of what is happening and not letting others change us gives us a certain degree of security.

> High jump coach A: *"Let's try out what happens when our athletes jump backwards over the pole."*
>
> High jump coach B: *"You're not the first to think of this. It won't work!"*

Person B, thus, retains control of what is happening, the price for which is that probably nothing new will develop. Good cooperation also means letting yourself be influenced by others, both practically and emotionally. Online, this is all the more important and motivating for good cooperation.

Conclusion for teamwork: Let yourself be influenced and changed by others, including emotionally (e.g. Coach B: *"Hey, that's a really cool idea! We could revolutionise the high jump with that!"*)

3.3 Exercises for teamwork online

Important prerequisites for real teamwork can be trained very well online. For existing teams, additional classroom workshops are important and necessary. If these are not possible, for example, due to time or local restrictions, it is also possible to fuse an existing team closer together online.

Getting to know each other

A surprising start that can help set the tone is often achieved with the following introduction exercise: Do not let the participants even introduce themselves with their actual education, professions and successes. Instead, suggest that they "carry away" themselves and the others into another world from the beginning. The following exercise is perfect for this, whether the participants already know each other well or not at all.

Exercise

Online "What Else Would I Have Liked to Become?"

All players think about what they would have liked to have done in their lives. All possibilities are open: for example, be the first woman on Mars, an organic farmer with five children, etc. The player then introduces themselves and speaks about their fictitious professional and private life. It's best to make sure that these invented lives are not chosen randomly, but have to do with the respective people themselves. They may be an earlier dream of a profession, a certain talent, a lapsed interest, etc., which are allowed to come on stage in this context.

TECHNOLOGY

- All participants switch to speaker view.
- If desired, a player can change their camera settings so that they do not see themselves.

And here are other exercises, which are also suitable for use in large groups:

Exercise

Online "Finding Things in Common"

At the start, all participants turn off their camera. One player starts spontaneously, turns on their camera and says something about themselves, for example: "*I like to ride my bike.*" All fellow players who also enjoy cycling turn on their camera as a sign of agreement as well. Similarities discovered in this way often arouse increased interest in each other and stimulate joint learning.

You can also do this exercise with professional statements only, for example: "*I like to be with customers*" or "*I often feel stressed*" or "*I get too many emails.*"

Exercise

Online "Speed Dating"

The participants are divided into breakout sessions of three people and discuss a given question for three minutes. After three minutes, new groups of three are formed to exchange views on another issue. Questions could include:

- What would you do if you didn't have to work for money?
- What would your best friends say about you if you weren't there?
- What's your passion?

TECHNOLOGY

- Breakout sessions: Groups of three

Exercise

Online "Two Truths"

The participants are sent into breakout sessions of three or four people. One person begins, telling a truth and an untruth about themselves. The others must guess which is true.

TECHNOLOGY

- Breakout sessions

Movement and activation exercises

To be and remain motivated and active online, movement is important. Hosts, moderators, managers, etc., are responsible for the regular physical "activation" of participants, especially during long online sessions.

Exercise

Online "Whac-A-Mole"

One volunteer stays in the Zoom window, while all other participants disappear out of the Zoom window by leaning to the side. Gradually, participants come back into the picture and make a repetitive movement there. The volunteer must now replicate these movements as soon as possible and say the name of the respective person, at which point the person disappears from the picture again. The goal is to make everyone disappear as soon as possible.

Exercise

Online "Follow the Leader"

Here, music is played and a participant (the "leader") starts to move to the music. The other participants follow these movements. The leader then says the name of another participant, who takes on the role of a leader and moves to the music and so on.

TECHNOLOGY

• Music is to be played for this exercise. (e.g. Pata, Pata by Miriam Makeba.)

The "Yes, and . . . " principle in a team

With this exercise, you can train listening:

Exercise

Online "Last Word/First Word"

The participants go together into breakout sessions and have a conversation on a given topic (suggested by the others). The last word of player A is always the first word of player B. To do this, the players have to listen to the end and thus cannot already prepare what they want to say themselves while the preceding person is speaking.

TECHNOLOGY

• Breakout sessions: partner work

Take over leadership and let yourself be guided

Joint leadership is the basis of real teamwork and each jointly improvised story on stage. Many exercises require assuming the role of a leader and giving it up again:

Exercise

Online "One-Word Stories"

Participants are given numbers, and the player with the number 1 begins a joint story by saying the first word. Number 2 says the second word of the story, etc. With nouns or verbs, the plot is further developed with adjectives decorating the story and filler words connecting the whole. At certain points in the story, one has to take the lead and, for example, determine the further development of the plot with a noun. At this point, quite a few people feel inhibited about taking on significant influence and thus a lot of responsibility for the story. In other places, however, no noun is required, and the player just needs to either decorate or connect. Here, though, other participants tend to have trouble because they do not like to be led.

TECHNOLOGY

• Each player receives a number, so an order is set.

And here's another exercise:

Exercise

Online "Press Conference"

Four players leave their cameras on, while all the others turn theirs off and become journalists at an online press conference. The visible players are a successful group, but they don't know what they've become successful with or what connects them. The journalists from the audience ask them as open questions as possible: for example, *"What was your most recent success?", "What are your next projects?", "What is the secret of your success?"* and always mention the name of the person they want to address, so that they are not confused.

The players answer these questions and define, bit by bit, what group they are. Anything is possible: a rock band, the first humans on Mars, etc. It is important that no one player dictates everything on their own, but that the joint story develops piece by piece. Here, presence, attention and listening are practised in order to be able to build on the offers of others creatively.

TECHNOLOGY

- All spectators turn off their cameras so that only the four players are visible. To do this, all participants must select "Hide Non-Video Participants" in their video settings.
- If they want, players can change their camera settings so they can't see themselves.

Exchange and transfer

At the end of a workshop, it is important to review the day and exchange what everyone has learned. If fatigue has set in towards the end, the following exercise is excellent:

Exercise

Online "Walk and Talk"

Here, first of all, pairs are formed. One participant then calls the other on their mobile, and both go for a walk – connected via their mobiles. On this walk, the two exchange ideas about the day. The best way to do this is to use the breakout sessions to form the pairs, and the participants exchange their numbers there. If participants do not want to give their number, they can exchange ideas in the breakout sessions instead. If there are an odd number of participants, a group of three must come together in a breakout session anyway.

TECHNOLOGY

- Phone calls via mobile

3.4   Improvised role-playing games online

I use this kind of improvised role-playing games very often in my classroom lessons, but they are also very useful online. Here are two examples from my online courses:

Provide critical feedback

All players turn off their cameras, except for two volunteers. In order for only the active players to be visible, everyone must select "Hide Non-Video Participants" setting. This role-playing game is about critical feedback, whereby one player has to give critical/negative feedback to the other. This can be feedback from a supervisor to an employee or feedback between two colleagues.

The audience decides what the employee did "wrong," or what an employee did to annoy their colleague (e.g. being late). Then, the two players play this situation. It's not about doing everything "right," but about just trying it out. In order to increase the difficulty, in a second round, you can also give the feedback recipient the task of not simply accepting the feedback, but justifying themselves and showing no understanding.

After the role-playing game, the feedback provider receives feedback from the viewers – What went well? What could they have done better? What else could they try? When suggestions come, I ask this person to try it out for themselves and jump into the role of a feedback provider. Depending on the group, I also slip into this role myself. Then, there is more feedback from the viewers. It's nice when different people jump into this role and different strategies become visible. In most cases, there's not one right way, but various promising approaches.

Dealing with difficult conversational situations

In breakout sessions with four participants each, the most current, tricky conversation situations are brought to the (virtual) table. Then, each group agrees on one situation and plays it out for the others. In order to do this, it must be clarified in advance who takes on what role, whereby the person who suggested the situation should always play themselves. That person shouldn't now try to master the situation particularly professionally; it's best if they behave as they actually did in the real situation.

After the scene, there is feedback from the participants, the viewers and me. I place a special focus on the topics "Yes, and . . . " and "status behaviour" (see chapter on status). Again, I proceed in such a way that participants who suggest different behaviours are encouraged to jump into this role immediately and just try it out. And again, they receive feedback for the various solution strategies that emerge and, if necessary, I slip into this role myself.

Chapter 4

Storytelling

4.1 Introduction to storytelling

Imagine yourself in the following situation: You want to buy a new car of a certain brand and have collected all the facts for a certain model. Your best friend tells you that he recently bought this exact car, and that it's "*reee-aaally baaaad*": In the very first year, the car had had to go to the workshop three times for expensive repairs. Once he even ended up stranded in the middle of the motorway – he would never buy a car from this maker again.

So, you now have a detailed list of facts about why this brand, this model is right for you. And you have your friend's story pulling you exactly in the opposite direction, namely not to buy this car under any circumstances. Does this story count only as individual additional information? Or do you let it influence you more deeply as to whether to buy that car? Probably the latter – and that's the power of storytelling!

Storytelling effectively and efficiently conveys explicit and implicit knowledge in the form of stories and has been used for some time in companies, in training, in advertising or in psychotherapy.

Information conveyed through stories reaches listeners directly and remains in the memory. Storytelling for knowledge transfer has also proven to be very helpful in educational contexts. Gestalt theory explains this by the fact that stories form a "whole," in which the participants find themselves comparatively easily from their own experience, in which they orient themselves and with which they can identify. In addition, people love to recount exciting stories again and again, which of course increases their reach.

I use storytelling in my seminars as follows:

1   I tell my own stories to convey content in an exciting and vivid way.
2   I get participants to tell stories from their lives so that they can combine what they have learned with what they have experienced and get to know each other better.

DOI: 10.4324/9781003172765-4

3   I communicate how to build stories and give participants feedback on their stories.
4   In team development, I get the team members to develop stories together and see where there are blockages in cooperation.

As a trainer, I like to tell stories from my own workshops. Sometimes, even private things (e.g. experiences with my teenage sons) to illustrate the important points of what I'm saying. On the one hand, I talk about difficult experiences (e.g. a challenging case of team development) and how I have handled them successfully. On the other hand, I also talk about mistakes and failures. If I can talk about my failures and laugh about them, it's a good way to build trust through openness – a rare commodity, especially online.

In improvisational theatre, stories are invented as a joint effort, in the moment. To do this, it is necessary for the players to know how stories are structured, that real teamwork is required and that they should focus less on their own egos, but on the story.

Stories take you into other worlds and are thus a wonderful key to creativity (Figure 4.1).

Figure 4. 1 © Evi Fill

4.2   Storytelling online

Online, we have a reduced direct effect on each other compared to events where we're physically present. This is because only part of our body language is visible. This makes stories all the more important! Their effect is amazing online, and they are therefore well suited because they help to overcome psychological distance and build closeness and trust. Personal and true stories are of particular importance. On the one hand, the more personal and emotional a story is, the greater the risk because we make ourselves vulnerable. On the other hand, however, the impact of an authentic story is potentially higher – and, as a result, the trust that can grow from it. However, it is always important not to overwhelm your audience and to adapt the degree of openness to the situation and the listeners.

According to Tom Salinsky (2020), the founder of the London improvisational theatre group "The Spontaneity Shop," storytelling has great qualities that can compensate for many disadvantages of online communication:

- Stories are conversation starters.
- Stories are engaging.
- Storytelling is innate.
- Stories are influential.
- Stories are vehicles for emotions.
- Stories are memorable.
- Stories are about change.

The following exercise lets participants experience these qualities directly: Two people (A and B) are first sent to a breakout session. There, A tells a true and personal story to the other person, B. Person B just listens, doesn't ask questions and doesn't tell a story of their own. The breakout sessions are terminated and an activity of about 10 minutes follows. Now, the original pairs are sent back together. Then, Person B tells the story of A, as far as they can remember. It's amazing in how much detail most stories can be retold! What is also interesting for A is what exactly has been remembered. Most of the time, the story becomes more compact, and abstract details will not have stuck.

Storytelling is therefore also widely used on the internet – for example, under the term "digital storytelling." Interactive forms, for example, with photos and videos, are used with the aim of spreading stories. Digital storytelling is often used for marketing purposes, for example, by asking for user stories.

It is important that the stories are compact. Especially online, this is crucial because the attention span is shorter than in face-to-face situations. Reducing stories to the essentials can be trained by trying to tell the story in half the time and then in half the time again, and so on – until there are only three words left. These three words must contain the essence of the story. For Romeo and Juliet, for example, it could be the following three words: 1. love, 2. feud and 3. poison.

4.3   Building stories

According to Cossart (2015), the arc of tension in a story is created in the following way:

> An **acting main character** (i.e. the hero in the Hero's Journey).
> This character needs **a direction, a goal**.
> **Difficulties or conflicts** that arise and initially prevent the main character from achieving their goal.

The tension in a story arises from the fact that the main character does not reach their goal so easily. Internal resistances can stand in their way, such as "*I want to achieve something, but I'm not up to the job.*" Or there are conflicts with other close figures along the lines of "*I want to achieve something, but my family does not support me.*" Conflicts with institutions or laws are also possible: "*I want to achieve something, but institutions or existing rules stand in my way.*"

A simple structure makes it easier to invent and tell stories! The **"Story Spine"** by Kenn Adams offers good advice:

Here is an example:

Tab. 4. I "Story Spine" (Mod. from Adams, 2007, p. 27; Schinko-Fischli, 2019, p. 114)

The **beginning** establishes a routine:	"Once upon a time . . . " "Every day . . . "
The **event** breaks the routine:	"But one day . . . "
The **centre** shows the consequences and increases the tension:	"And that's why . . . " "And that's why . . . " "And that's why . . . " Repetition as often as necessary
The **climax** introduces the solution:	"Until finally . . . "
The **end** establishes a new routine:	"And since then . . . "

> *"Once upon a time there was an actor who loved the stage above all else. Every day he would look forward to the performance in the evening. But one day the Corona Lockdown came and he lost his work at the theatre, and his audience. And that's why he got into a deep crisis and no longer knew what to do with his life. And that's why he withdrew more and more and wondered if he wanted to live on. And that's why one evening he stood on the parapet of a bridge and was about to jump. Until finally he realised that his life was not over, and he wanted to help other people who are thinking of taking their own lives. So he came up with the idea of writing and performing a piece for depressed people. And since Corona passed, he has been performing his play 'The Bridge' in psychiatric hospitals and schools, and has already helped many people turn away from suicide."*

Stories always consist of cause and effect, so the Story Spine doesn't proceed with "then," but with "and that's why." Everything that happens in a story happens for a reason. What happens at the beginning of a story must therefore be given meaning later on. In the case of invented stories in improvisational theatre, the art is to remember as much as possible and to reincorporate this material into the story later. If the main character of a story wears a scarf at the beginning, for example, it can later be the murder tool or the solution to the problem. This reintegration really rounds up stories.

Here is a more detailed description of the structure of a story:

1   The beginning establishes the routine

At the beginning, the main character is introduced. We get to know the main character and start to identify with it/them. Only identification makes a story really exciting.

Imagine the following beginnings of a story:

> *"Andrea is crossing the road, when suddenly a car comes towards her."*
>
> *"Andrea is pregnant and is crossing the road, when suddenly a car comes towards her."*
>
> *"Andrea is six months pregnant, and she has already had several miscarriages. She has another appointment with the gynaecologist after work. As she's walking across the road, a car suddenly comes towards her."*

The more we know about Andrea, the more interesting the story becomes. And the longer the basis is, the longer the story will last after that.

2   The event breaks the routine

Once the basis is established, the routine must be broken. In Andrea's story, the event is the car that comes towards her. The so-called "promise" is already visible here. The promise is always a yes/no question. When this is answered and the promise is fulfilled, the story is over. In Andrea's story, the promise is: Does the unborn child survive or not?

The fundamental promise of stories is always the question of whether there will be a happy ending or not.

3   The centre shows the consequences and increases the tension

But before the story comes to an end, consequences must be shown and the tension increased. It is important to make the problem worse first, so that the tension can rise and the audience wants to know what happens next.

> *"Andrea is six months pregnant, and she has already had several miscarriages. She has another appointment with the gynaecologist after work. As she's walking across the road, a car suddenly comes towards her. It's already dark and the motorist obviously doesn't see her. Andrea freezes and can no longer get out of the way. The car catches her sideways, so violently that she is thrown through the air. Andrea sees her life flash before her eyes, and her only wish is that the baby inside her survives."*

4   The climax introduces the solution

> *"She falls on the verge on the side of the road and remains unconscious. Passers-by and the motorist rush to her. A little later the ambulance arrives and takes her to hospital."*

5   The end establishes a new routine

> *"Andrea wakes up in hospital and has pain in her right leg – it's probably broken. She puts her hands on her belly and feels that the baby is still alive. A little later the doctor comes and informs Andrea that although her leg is broken, the baby is doing well. Andrea is overjoyed, and knows how valuable every minute with this child is and will be."*

Incidentally, this procedure also applies to true stories. These are not primarily about retelling them in as much detail and realistically as possible, but rather about building the story in an exciting way. Too many details come at the expense of the story and usually generate boredom. For true stories too, it is therefore important to reduce the storyline to the central elements and to equip the story with a good arc of tension.

For example, in 2004, I was fired (true), which in itself does not make for a particularly exciting story:

> *"At the beginning of the new millennium, I worked for a few years at a company in the health sector. I enjoyed the job. Then my head of division got a new job and a colleague of mine took over. The first thing he did was fire me. After that, I set up my own business."*

Here's what the story looks like once I've built it up according to the Story Spine:

> *"In 2004 I was 32 years old and employed by a company in the health sector. It was a small business and I felt very comfortable there. My colleagues were also my friends. Overall, I felt like I had finally arrived in my life.* (Basis) *Then the head of division moved to another company. One of my colleagues took over the vacant position and informed me shortly afterwards that he would 'release' me.* (Event breaks the routine) *As a reason, he explained that my position would no longer be needed in the future. That pulled the rug from under my feet and I didn't know what else I could do. In my last team meeting I was in the meeting room with the whole team; sitting on the red sofa, I could feel the tears coming down. But it got worse, because it gradually became clear that my ex-colleague and new boss had lied to me, and had already hired a successor to take my job – before I was even gone!* (Increase tension) *Partly because of this deep insult, and after a little time, I decided to set up my own business. In retrospect, this was the best professional decision and I'm basically glad I got this 'push' – even if it felt like a brutal kick at the time."* (New routine)

The message of the story is clear: crises can make us stronger.

Please don't tell such a story if you actually have to dismiss someone yourself! You could tell the story if a colleague of yours got fired.

Each effective true story also contains the following elements:

1   *Story*: The plot of the story must be driven forwards in order to build up the tension
2   *Colour*: At certain points in the story, sensual details are also needed – How did it smell there? How did it feel? What was the weather like? – so that you can put yourself in the situation
3   *Emotion*: A good story transmits emotions! It helps to describe one's own feelings vividly

Many personal stories are boring because too little attention is paid to these points. It is classic that there are too many details and the plot isn't driven forward. Who hasn't found themselves bored by such a story? However, if there are no details at all in a story, and only the plot is told, this means that we cannot put ourselves into the situation, and we can't build a mental picture. Emotions are the salt in the soup – which is the great advantage of telling stories instead of merely relating facts.

Breakout sessions are particularly good for getting across our own emotionality, when we tell a true story. We can operate a kind of "remote control" with three buttons: story (the plot must be driven forward), colour (the story must be decorated) and emotion (emotions should be described). This is a playful way to pep up a story.

In summary, according to Tom Salinsky (2020), we can say the following:

*   Identify the spine, the central idea of the story.
*   Work out the structure of your story.
*   Be ruthless about leaving out what isn't needed.
*   Emphasise people, emotions and cause and effect.
*   Use visual language and tell some details.
*   Protect surprises and use anticipation.
*   Use examples and look for contrasts.
*   And, last but not least, practise your story.

4.4   The message of stories

It is important that the narrator understands what is to be achieved with a story and what must therefore be the message of the story. With each story, values are also conveyed. For example, if we want to tell the story of our company, we will almost inevitably try to convey the company's values. This message does not always have to be expressly formulated, but is conveyed "along the way."

Sometimes, however, stories have a different effect than the one originally planned. For example, stories are often used to convince employees of something. Here is an example from one of my workshops. An executive of a large Swiss insurance company had initiated a change process to introduce flat hierarchies and agile work in his department. His team was still sceptical and resistant to this change. So, he wanted to tell a personal story at the next online meeting (a real meeting was not possible at that time):

> *"It was a few years ago when I made a big trip with my wife for the first time. We flew together to Mexico . . . it was a long flight and we arrived late and very tired in Guadalajara. When we finally got out of the airport hall, it was just after midnight, and there were no taxis. My wife and I sat on the sidewalk exhausted and didn't know what was going on. Suddenly a man came up to us, spoke to us kindly and offered to take us with him; he said he could also offer us a room. We were very unsure what this meant and what was behind it. But in the end, we went along with it. This man took us with his car, and we stayed with him and his wife in their house. They invited us to eat with them, and eventually we stayed there for three nights, and have remained friends with him and his family to this day. What I mean by this is: It can be worthwhile to get involved in the unknown and just try it out!"*

I find the use of such stories in this context questionable. On the one hand, the intention is all too obvious, and who likes to be persuaded by something against their will? In this respect, I recommend the use of stories in the business context less as a medium for changing attitudes or convictions, but much more as a conversation opener.

Accordingly, this story could have been used as follows:

> *" . . . Suddenly a man came up to us, spoke to us kindly and offered to take us with him; he said could also offer us a room. We were very unsure what this meant and what was behind it. I have the impression that you are now feeling the same about this change process. I see many questions, maybe doubts, in your faces. What will it mean for you? What do you think about me and this project?"*

After an open exchange about it, the manager could tell the story to the end.

Precisely because stories have a potentially big impact, in these days of fake news, it is important that storytelling is not used to manipulate employees! Stories must be used responsibly and consciously, and we need to know what we want to achieve. For example, we may wish to:

- win over the listeners for an idea
- start an open conversation
- illustrate an abstract theme
- reveal something of ourselves to enable openness and trust

Another use of storytelling in companies is to tell stories together. The gain here is that the end and moral of the story are not fixed from the outset; rather, the future is invented or developed jointly in a co-creative process. This requires a common structure of the kind offered, for example, by the "Hero's Journey."

4.5 The Hero's Journey

Joseph Campbell explored the myths of humanity in search of universal structures of human life and thus developed the idea of the Hero's Journey. The Hero's Journey has an archetypal basic structure and shows an ideal development and maturation process of a human being. Christoph Vogler simplified this structure and became very influential with it in Hollywood. Countless books (e.g. the Harry Potter series by J. K. Rowling) and films (e.g. the Star Wars films by George Lucas) are based on the structure of the Hero's Journey.

The Hero's Journey follows an inner script:

The familiar world: The hero lives their everyday life. They are often something of an outsider with a vague feeling that there must be more out there.

The call to adventure: The feeling that something is missing, combined with a brief insight into an unfamiliar world, make our hero think about heading off into an adventure.

Denial of the call: The hero ignores the call to adventure because they are afraid of the unknown.

Meeting with the mentor: A mentor comes into play and stands by the hero.

Crossing the first threshold: The mentor helps the hero to cross the first threshold into the unfamiliar world.

Trials, allies, enemies: The hero has to find their way around the new world, meeting friends and enemies.

Entering the deepest cave: The hero meets their greatest opponents and also recognises their greatest inner enemy.

Struggling with a decision: In the decisive live-or-die battle, the hero also confronts their own "dark side" – but conquers it.

Reward and taking up the sword: The hero has changed, and their "new self" heads back to their old world.

Homecoming: With these new experiences and insights, the hero returns to their old world.

Renewal and transformation: The hero can now bring what they have learned into everyday life and thus help others.

Return with the elixir: The elixir consists of integrating what has been learned into everyday life, enriching the hero's life and making it easier.

The hero is actually a normal person. But what makes them so special is their courage to face up to difficulties and thereby change themselves and their world for the better. For many people, these stories of change offer an attractive surface onto which they can project their own development processes. The more a person's own desires, longings and developmental needs resonate in the story, the greater the level of identification, and the more captivating the story is.

4.6   Using the Hero's Journey

Hero's Journeys are not only used in psychotherapy (Paul Rebillot) but also very well suited to helping teams find their way, in both analogue and digital contexts. Here, too, the following applies: For team development, face-to-face workshops are superior to online events and thus remain the first choice. But if it is not possible to gather the team in one place for important reasons (and by that I do not mean reasons of cost), then team development online has its place.

Hero's Journey online – team development

First, I get the team familiar with the structure of the Hero's Journey. Then, I divide the team into two groups and get each group to set down the Hero's Journey of their own team in breakout sessions (e.g. on a whiteboard). Each group should determine at which point in the Hero's Journey the team is currently standing, and how it can successfully meet the next challenges. It is also interesting to see whether the two groups agree and to compare these two perspectives. With the help of the Hero's Journey, a team can step back a little and look at their own situation from a different, hopefully more accessible, point of view. In addition, a discussion arises about where you are in the process of change and what it takes to successfully overcome blockages, difficulties, etc.

Hero's Journey offline – managers

In autumn 2018, I went over a Hero's Journey with the executives of an international security company in a face-to-face workshop. A few years previously, a department in the company had realised that it was necessary to develop new software, even though the old version was still selling very well. But they wanted to stay ahead of the competition and fit for the future, so the next step was already necessary (call to adventure). With the vital support of a member of the management (mentor), the department set out to develop the new software (crossing the first threshold). This task proved to be very complex, and the new product initially had more weaknesses than the old software, which was already well established (trials, allies, enemies). Nevertheless, it was clear that this new software would be the future and would have much more potential after the bugs were fixed. However, some customers were already disappointed, and there was a risk that new customers would no longer want the new product. Big investments and the future of the department were at stake. In the meantime, the criticism within the company had also grown in intensity (entering the deepest cave).

The workshop took place with the management team, which we split into halves. Both groups agreed that the team was on the verge of a "decisive battle." In the course of the discussion, it became clear that only one thing was needed to win this battle: the belief in oneself and in one's own product (elixir).

Hero's Journey – performance skills

The Hero's Journey is very suitable for seminars on the topic of performance competence. There I let the participants tell a personal Hero's Journey around the key question "What great difficulties have you overcome in life, and how did you do that?" Often stories cover professional changes or other pivotal life events. Participants receive feedback on their Hero's Journey, which can be done either online or offline. Online, however, the stories should be kept really short! Feedback is useful on the one hand with regard to the structure of the story, but on the other hand also in terms of its effect.

In a further step, I like to ask the participants how much risk they have taken with their story. This clearly shows the great effect of openness that is appropriate to the situation. Those who have not been personal enough and have taken too little risk often receive the feedback that the story is rather less captivating and probably less memorable. Too much openness, on the other hand, can also overwhelm the audience, but this happens very rarely.

4.7   Exercises for storytelling online

Stories can also be built up and used in online training in an exciting way!

Stories of the participants

The following exercise is very suitable for starting a seminar on any topic:

Exercise

True Stories from a Keyword

Here, you form groups of three, and one person says any keyword, after which another tells a short, true and personal story based on it. By the end, everyone will have told a short story about themselves.

TECHNOLOGY

- Breakout sessions: groups of three

Exercise

My Hero's Journey

The participants introduce each other through a little Hero's Journey, describing the obstacles that they have had to be overcome in life. It is important to pay attention to the tension arc of the story and to increase the drama of the difficulties, before dissolving the tension again. Not all stages of the Hero's Journey are necessary – the basic structure is sufficient. Online, the stories need to be kept short.

TECHNOLOGY

- All participants switch to speaker view.
- The active player can change their camera setting if they do not wish to see themselves.

Building stories

In order to tell exciting stories, you need to know how stories are structured in principle, and practise them until storytelling becomes natural. The following exercises are suitable for this purpose:

Exercise

Story Spine

Demonstrate the exercise first with a participant, then send everyone into pairs in breakout sessions. Each pair should tell each other stories with the help of Adams's "Story Spine." The sentence beginnings are given in each case.

With the help of the Story Spine, it is also possible to work very well on existing stories. The Story Spine helps to structure the story and shape it in an exciting way.

"Once upon a time . . ."
"Every day . . ."
" But one day . . ."
"And that's why . . ."
"And that's why . . ."
"And that's why . . ."
"Until finally . . ."
"And since then . . ."

TECHNOLOGY

- Breakout sessions: partner work

Exercise

Three-Sentence Stories

Demonstrate the exercise with two participants, then send the participants into groups of three in breakout sessions. Each group of three invents a story together that consists of only three sentences. One player starts the story with the first sentence, the second adds the middle sentence – which is the centre of the story, including its challenge – and the third player concludes the story with the final sentence.

TECHNOLOGY

- Breakout sessions: groups of three

Exercise

Increasing the Risk

The exercise is demonstrated, then participants go into breakout sessions, in groups of three:

> Player 1 starts with the beginning of a story, then Players 2 and 3 increase the risk, for example:
> Player 1: *"Sabine fell head over heels in love with Thomas."*
> Player 2: *"Thomas is married and has two children."*
> Player 3: *"Sabine is 40 and would like to have a child."*

TECHNOLOGY

- Breakout sessions: groups of three

Exercise

Story, Colour, Emotion

The exercise is demonstrated, then participants go into breakout sessions, in pairs. One person begins to tell a personal story.

The other has a kind of remote control in their hand and can say "story," "colour" or "emotion" at any time. The narrator then has to adjust their story and either advance the plot, go into more detail or describe emotions. Afterwards, they can give each other feedback.

TECHNOLOGY

• Breakout sessions: partner work

Stories of collaboration

As already described, stories are very suitable to see where the blockage in the collaboration is. This is possible with the following exercises:

Exercise

One-Sentence Stories

The players jointly compose a story, one sentence at a time. Player 1 starts with the first sentence, Player 2 continues with the second sentence, etc. The story can actually be made up of multiple sentences, but the players must take turns contributing them, one at a time. Here, we can often observe many dimensions and or perhaps blockages in the collaborative work: whether offers are heard and taken up, who has trouble taking the lead and opening themselves up to making mistakes, etc. Or, for example, some may not wish to be guided and are unable to let go of their own ideas if the story evolves in a different direction. Based on the quality of the story, one can discuss together what has worked well in cooperation and what went less well.

TECHNOLOGY

• Each player receives a number to establish an order.

Chapter 5

Status and image

5.1 Introduction to status behaviour

The term "status" is used in different contexts and has several meanings. Social status means the position of a person or group within society. Keith Johnstone (1979) paid a lot of attention to teaching actors about their status behaviour. He found that scenes on stage became much more exciting and realistic when the actors took on a certain status. This status behaviour is partly independent of social status and can be influenced and changed. This is the exciting thing about this concept and an important focus of my teaching: being able to adapt our own status behaviour to the situation.

We constantly display our own status not only through our body language and verbal language but also through how we relate to space and time. Our status adapts constantly in relation to others, changing from moment to moment. For example, as soon as someone has some sort of accident, their status drops. Depending on their handling of the mishap, their status can recover quickly, for example, if they remain calm and composed, or even turn the situation to their own advantage.

High and low status have different qualities and are appropriate in different situations. It is very important to convey to the participants that high-status behaviour is not necessarily the key to success.

Low status

Low status is conveyed in everyday life with the following signals:

- standing on one leg or with the legs crossed
- tilting the head to the side

DOI: 10.4324/9781003172765-5

- making ourselves small and taking up little space
- adopting a closed posture
- not holding eye contact, looking away first
- making agitated and twitchy movements
- touching oneself, especially on the head and face

It always depends on the situation, the behaviour of the other person and our own attitude.

Low-status behaviour often also has an amusing aspect. This can be seen in workshops, when everyone finds themselves laughing at a low-status figure. One profession even thrives on playing the low-status game, namely comedians and clowns. They are paid to lower their own status and laugh at it. In life, we usually don't laugh at low-status behaviour, otherwise the person in question may lose face. But we like to watch mishaps and failures on television and on the internet in the knowledge that no one can hear our laughter.

High status

Typical high-status signals include:

- a wide stance, equally on both legs
- holding the head straight and moving it little
- upright and open posture
- eye contact is maintained
- big and calm gestures
- touching others – the further up the body (arm, shoulder and head), the more the status of the counterpart decreases
- taking up a lot of room and positioning oneself in the middle of a given space

Many politicians and managers love playing a high-status role and are specially trained for it. In press photos, they especially use the way they touch others very specifically in order to appear as superior as possible. Such people touch each other less out of affection, than a chance to score in these power plays.

Emmanuel Macron was specifically trained for his first meeting with Donald Trump, squeezing Trump's hand very hard to clarify his own high status right at the start.

Status flexibility

We habitually prefer to assume a particular status without being aware of it. This gives us a certain range of status behaviour, where we feel most comfortable. One aim of my workshops is to gain an awareness of our own status behaviour and to increase the range of behavioural possibilities.

High-status behaviour means that we have a potentially higher level of assertiveness, radiate more authority and are taken more seriously by others. However, we may take space from others, get less honest feedback and create more competitive situations.

Low-status behaviour allows others to get more space, we're perceived as being more empathetic and sympathetic and can increase the status of others. The drawbacks are that we tend to be less assertive and less heard and seen.

High- and low-status behaviours are therefore appropriate in different situations.

There are four ways to change our status: (Schinko-Fischli, 2019, p. 89)

1   We can raise our own status by, for example, telling a success story
2   We can raise our own status by lowering the status of others, for example, through criticism
3   We can lower our own status, for example, through self-criticism
4   We can lower our own status by raising the status of others, for example, through recognition and admiration.

Another way to significantly raise our own status is to take the conversation to a meta level. On this level, the current situation is observed "from a bird's-eye view," and from here, we can reflect. For example, this is possible when reflecting on processes in team sessions. If we have the courage to speak about our meta-observations (e.g. if we're often interrupted, or when conflicts are played out subliminally), then we can not only influence the situation but also raise our status.

Of course, our own status behaviour also has a lot to do with self-confidence. Low-status behaviour often arises from an internal uncertainty, and high-status behaviour does not seem credible if it is only played outwardly. At this point, participants will often object, saying that they want to remain authentic. Of course, professionally guided learning settings must be about reconciling the participants' learning process with their personality. However – assuming that individual status behaviour has been socially learned in the course of development

– it can also be changed, expanded and, above all, made more flexible. Experience shows that newly learned behaviours feel quite "normal" after a certain period of time and therefore authentic. It is important that the participants take responsibility for learning in the area of their own status behaviour, identify the scope for learning themselves and make their own decisions in which direction they want to develop their status behaviour.

Status in sales

More generally, it can be said that a seller should place their status a little below that of the customer. In contrast to the status towards the customer, a seller can bring the attractiveness of the product to the fore by taking on a high status over the product! For example, a car salesman can have a very high status over "his" cars, but he has to lower his status slightly compared to the customer.

Similarly, in a job interview, it is ideal if one's own status is a trace below that of the interviewer. The applicant can take a high status in terms of their qualifications, but they must lower their status towards the interviewer. Here, too, status flexibility is required because it depends on the status of the other person.

Status and women

Women are still often brought up to adopt a lower status and to take up little space. Typical female behaviours – inclining the head, crossing the legs, touching our own hair or face, etc. – have the effect of lowering status. Woe betide a woman who significantly raises her status behaviour! She'll be quickly criticised for this.

Closeness among women often arises from self-criticism and self-devaluation. If a woman is bold enough not to play this game and takes on a high status, she risks losing that closeness and even being excluded from the feeling of solidarity among other women.

5.2   Status online

Videoconferencing, online meetings and online workshops significantly influence status behaviour or negotiation of status in interactions because there are fewer means available to make our own status clear! For example, taller people cannot take advantage of their height online because physical size no longer plays a role. Status symbols (watches, clothing, etc.) also have less influence online. We can't touch others and they can't touch us, so these classic status games are not available to us.

Nevertheless, status games and battles do not simply disappear online. They are only played out differently. For example, there are online platforms where only a few people are visible – the ones who speak the most. The others aren't seen at all. The difference in status can hardly be illustrated more clearly.

Status behaviour online

Online, each person usually has only their own video window in which to display their status. This window is the same size for everyone. Nevertheless, there are certainly opportunities to play the game here! For example, we can take up more space by working with visible gestures or getting our face closer to the camera, filling more space – and showing a higher status.

Lowering our status online is easy, by holding the head slanted, touching our own face or head, moving away from the camera and taking up little space in the video window or by being too low in the frame.

Even more than in normal meetings, a conversation can be dominated online by participants who "have the floor" for a long time. With the "Speaker view" setting, the main speakers are then highly visible. While it's possible to attract a lot of attention offline through silence and non-verbal high-status behaviour, this is much more difficult online.

Group dynamic aspects are also to some extent eliminated or, if possible, carried out via private chat (e.g. *"Are you also bored with this?" "He always says the same thing."*). It is not possible to look at each other online and communicate directly non-verbally.

The host or moderator has a strong position online and can significantly influence proceedings. For example, in many meetings, you have to raise your hand first, then the host/moderator gives you the floor and only then are you allowed to speak. Such methods lower the status of the participants – with consequences for their basic feelings in the seminar and the learning process. For this reason, I prefer to work in small groups and do not give the floor to anyone, but make it possible for all participants to jump in and take part at any time. This also creates a certain vibrancy online. The easiest way to achieve this is when all microphones are switched on continuously.

Low-status online

Online, low status is communicated as follows:

Head posture	The head is tilted to the side
Body posture	Video window is not filled enough
Movements	Twitchy and nervous gestures
Touches	Touching ourselves, especially on the face and head
Language	Many "um," "er" or other filler words Hesitation Allowing ourselves to be interrupted Criticising ourselves Defending ourselves ("*I had no choice.*") Using vague auxiliary verbs ("*I would,*" "*I should,*" "*I could*") Frequently using reinforcing adverbs (*very, definitely, completely,* ...) or filling adverbs (*of course, naturally* ...)
Background	Untidy and cluttered Private and personal items (unusual pictures, the kids' handicrafts, etc.) Not a proper study or office room, but the kitchen, the living room or even the children's room

High-status online

High status is displayed online with the following signals:

Head posture	Straight head posture The head moves little
Body posture	Taking up a lot of space in the video window Upright and open posture
Movements	Calm and targeted movements Filling the space available with visible gestures
Touches	Not touching our face
Language	Speaking in whole sentences Inserting pauses Telling stories (storytelling!) Asking questions Interrupting others Judging others – criticising or praising! (Even by praising others, we still put ourselves above the other and thus increase our own status.) Avoiding vague auxiliary verbs and using stronger modal verbs ("*I will,*" "*I want,*" "*I can*")
Background	Tidy and as neutral as possible In an office at home or at work In the background, only work-relevant objects are visible or subtle optical stimuli

Status and space

The background is of great importance in online communication. Who's allowed to work in the real office and who is still in home office? Who has a proper working space at home and who is squashed into a corner of the kitchen? And what do you see in the background? A tidy working environment with many books or untidy shelves full of private objects? (Figure 5.1)

Status and time

Arriving too late, leaving early, making phone calls on the side and cancelling at short notice are all ways to make it clear that you have more important commitments than this meeting or that workshop. They clearly demonstrate high status and downgrade the other parties involved. This behaviour also works well online and can be observed in exactly the

Figure 5. 1 © Evi Fill

same way. Creating a binding and trusting online atmosphere is difficult and challenging. It is also important to be able to rely on the presence of the other parties involved.

5.3   Status paradox

In her book "*Spielend unterrichten und Kommunikation gestalten*" (playful teaching and communicating), Maike Plath describes an extremely interesting and practically valuable concept: the status paradox. Plath is a teacher and theatre trainer who has further developed the topic of status at a hotspot school in Berlin. She came to the following conclusion: The higher our self-confidence is (inside us), the more we can lower our status outwardly (how we appear to others). And the deeper you lower your status to the outside world, the greater the respect you receive from others (Plath, 2015).

Young people often try to lower the status of teachers in order to raise their own status in the class. The status game, as played by students, is to lower the status of the teacher against the teacher's will. However, it is something else if the teacher consciously decides to lower their own status as projected to the outside world, as this can increase other's respect for them.

Plath describes an example from her class with a young man who had tuned out and was no longer reachable: she knelt in front of this student (low status!) and sang "Yesterday" by the Beatles to him. She kept singing until the student couldn't take it anymore and had to laugh. His barriers came down and he cried out, "*OK, OK, Ms Plath, please stop! I'll do anything you say!*" From that moment on, the connection to this student was re-established.

With increasing experience and security, it is easier to lower the status we display to the outside world. In my workshops, I personally report on my own failures and am able to laugh about them. The interesting thing is that the feedback I receive says that this makes me come across as likeable, approachable and human and that as a trainer, I am perceived as all the more convincing and confident. Nevertheless, even authenticity in this regard is not a miracle cure, and in certain situations, it is very helpful to take a high status. Status flexibility is therefore crucial.

5.4   Hierarchy paradox

Social status in the form of a hierarchical position, for example, naturally influences personal status behaviour. From a high hierarchical position, it is easier to assert our interests and to assume a higher status.

Nevertheless, this status must also be secured with the appropriate status behaviour if necessary. Otherwise, there is a risk of losing authority or colleagues' recognition.

Lehner and Ötsch (2015) conclude that flat hierarchies lead to more status struggles. The reason for this is that your own status is no longer automatically protected by the hierarchical position in the company and must be constantly defended by your own high-status behaviour. One advantage of traditional hierarchies is obviously that one's own status does not constantly have to be renegotiated.

5.5   Appearance online

During online events, it seems that participants watch proceedings very closely and attentively. And because there are fewer immediately perceptible indications of status behaviour than in face-to-face events, what can be seen is examined all the more closely. There seems to be a widespread opinion that when we're online, it doesn't really matter what impressions our online presence leaves behind. This idea can come to those who are confronted on-screen with untidy rooms, inappropriate books on the shelf or large-format private photos of the beach holiday, etc., as part of their online work – that is, they see an unprofessional public appearance.

Camera and lighting

It is important that the camera is at eye level, so that the user has to look neither upwards nor downwards into it. This places the communication at the proverbial "eye-to-eye" level.

Good lighting is of course important. Light sources should not be behind the person in the picture, as backlighting is rarely a good option. Ideally, one is discreetly and evenly illuminated.

Image framing

The next step is favourable positioning in front of the camera. Here, care should be taken that not only the head but also a part of the upper body is visible, so that gestures can be seen. One tip is to frame yourself so that there is not too much space above your head. This automatically ensures that a part of the torso is also visible. It is not uncommon to see that the hands disappear completely from the picture. This is a pity because the hands offer a wide range of expressive possibilities, which support interaction or communication.

Background

I prefer "real" backgrounds and thus the insight into the real home office. However, this should give an appropriate impression of professionalism. Virtual backgrounds usually seem artificial and say little about our own personality. A peek into the home office can slightly lower the status, but it creates a certain closeness and facilitates confidence building ("You let me see who you are").

Eye contact

As already mentioned at the beginning, I focus my gaze on the participants and do not look straight into the camera. Their non-verbal feedback is very important to me because I can refer to it spontaneously and, if necessary, ask immediately, clarify uncertainties promptly or respond to statements of consent. Ideally, the camera is set in such a way that both are possible: to see the participants and to convey a feeling of direct eye contact.

Presence

Presence is a necessary prerequisite for actors and impro-actors and is a central theme in drama schools. Presence arises when we are completely in the moment, focused on it and open to what is happening all around. Even in face-to-face teaching, it's not so easy to achieve presence, and it's all the more difficult online because presence is conveyed very strongly through body language.

It certainly helps online if people aren't trying to do other things on the side. This means switching off the mail program, smartphone, etc! The impression of presence is reinforced when there is an immediate reaction to what is happening. Presence means, after all, being awake to interpersonal contact. That is why it is so essential online to use the comparatively sparse means and possibilities of virtual contact to develop sustainable working relationships.

Feedback on online presence

Seminars on the topic of presentation competence are essentially about providing participants with feedback on how they come across online. During a short introduction to the professional and personal background, I pay attention to the following:

- Does the physical background look "professional"?
- Is the camera at eye level?
- Is the head straight?

- Are the upper body and gestures visible?
- Are the hands touching the face or the head?
- Is the person sitting upright?
- Are they using humour?
- Are breaks taken?
- Is the length of the presentation appropriate?
- Are both professional (higher status) and personal (lower status) themes adressed?
- What does the voice sound like?
- Are many filler words used?
- Etc.

PowerPoint Karaoke

You can train your own spontaneity with regard to presentations online with the PowerPoint Karaoke exercise. This form was developed in 2006 by the "Central Intelligence Agency" in Berlin and has been very popular ever since. Actually, PowerPoint Karaoke is organised as a public event where volunteers give a presentation on completely unfamiliar PowerPoint slides.

To prepare for the exercise online, every participant looks for a Power-Point presentation on the internet. This should contain many pictures and not too much written information. Then one participant sends their PowerPoint presentation via the chat to the first volunteer. This person should never have seen the slides before. They open the document via the chat, share the screen and their spontaneous presentation can begin.

Another option is to use the Internet Portal for PowerPoint Karaoke (www.kapopo.de). There, free PowerPoint slides of different difficulty levels are offered online.

5.6   Exercises for status online

Training in status behaviour and status flexibility can be very effective online. The following exercise is particularly suitable as an introduction to the theme of status:

Exercise

Status Appearance

Send a player a number from 1 to 10 via chat (1 is the lowest status, 10 the highest). Then, the player must welcome the audience with the phrase *"Good evening ladies and gentlemen,"* applying and assuming this status as they do so. The viewers then guess which status number the player was given and give them feedback on how they appeared.

TECHNOLOGY

- All participants switch to speaker view.
- The status numbers are sent via the private chat.

Everyone has a certain status behaviour that makes them feel most comfortable, usually within a certain range. If we move outside of this area, we may no longer feel authentic, which is simply because it is unfamiliar. We can get to know our own comfort zone with the next exercise. Because this exercise can be very intense or even upsetting, it is important that only volunteers participate!

Exercise

Status Feedback

The player sits in front of the camera as neutrally as possible. The viewers give the person feedback on the status they perceive in numbers from 1 to 10 (1 = very low status, 10 = very high status). If desired, they can also say how they came to this assessment, that is which body-language signals raised or lowered the status. It is also interesting to think about what assessment you would like to hear, for example, the highest possible status.

TECHNOLOGY

- All participants switch to speaker view.
- The players can change their camera settings if they want so that they don't see themselves.

High- and low-status behaviour can be practised with the following exercise:

Exercise

Status Battles

Two players are given a situation by the audience, for example, two colleagues on an online call, two politicians in an online meeting or two friends in a private online meeting. Then, this scene is improvised by the two players, who must then fight for the highest or lowest status. From time to time, stop the scene and ask the viewers who currently has the higher or lower status, and why.

TECHNOLOGY

* All spectators turn off their cameras so that only the players are visible. To do this, all participants must select "Hide Non-Video Participants" in their video settings.

With the next exercise, status flexibility can be trained:

Exercise

Status See-saw

Two players improvise together a scene, whereby at the beginning, there is a clear status difference. For the first scene, I usually take an online job interview. The status gap is deliberately exaggerated. At the beginning of the scene, the head of personnel should have the highest possible status and the applicant as low as possible (the more extreme, the better). On a scale of 1–10 (1 = very low status, 10 = very high status), the manager should be a 10 and the applicant a 1. Once the (unequal) conversation has got going, the players can slowly start to see-saw, with each status changing slowly. The interviewer lowers their status, while the applicant slowly raises theirs. In the end, the manager should have the lowest possible status and the applicant the highest possible status. By the end, the manager usually ends up begging the applicant to please please please take the job. To trigger the swing in status, a good reason is needed, which the players come up with on the spot. For example, it turns out that the applicant is the son of the company owner or has spicy information about the head of personnel, etc., but only later comes out with it.

TECHNOLOGY

- All viewers turn off their cameras so that only the players are visible. To do this, all participants must select "Hide Non-Video Participants" in their video settings.

Exercise

Status Meeting

Four volunteers improvise a team meeting with each other (the company or organisation is specified by the audience). Via the chat, the host gives each of the four players a status number from 1 to 4, with each number only assigned once. Everyone knows their own status, but not the status of the others. Afterwards, the audience estimates which numbers were sent to the four players.

TECHNOLOGY

- All viewers turn off their cameras so that only the players are visible. To do this, all participants must select "Hide Non-Video Participantso" in their video settings.

Exercise

Guessing Status

This exercise requires four or five volunteers, with everyone else watching. The host allocates each player a status number between 1 and 8 (1 = lowest status, 8 = highest status) but doesn't tell the players which number, so that they do not know their own status. However, the other players *are* informed of it, as follows: the host sends one player to the waiting room and tells the others that player's status number. It's best if they write it down. This process is repeated until all the players know the status numbers of all the others but not their own status. Then follows a short role-playing game under the title "Team Session," and the viewers decide which company it is and which topic the volunteers are to discuss.

The "meeting" begins, and the volunteers are instructed to treat the other "meeting participants" according to the status they've been allocated. Essentially, this means acting with low status towards those with higher status and assuming high status when interacting with participants who have been allocated low status. Over time, the behaviour of the others should give each person a sense of what status they themselves have been allocated. They are likely to begin behaving accordingly.

At the end, all players estimate which status number they probably got. Then, the actual given numbers are revealed. The evaluation includes how close the role players have come to the status allocated to them, how they felt in their respective roles and any further thoughts or feedback from the viewers.

TECHNOLOGY

- All viewers turn off their cameras so that only the players are visible. To do this, all participants must select "Hide Non-Video Participantso" in their video settings.

5.7   Exercises for appearance online

The following are some exercises that can be used to work on our own "performance" skills, especially making presentations more effective. Many of the exercises are equally suitable for online seminars and face-to-face workshops.

Exercise

Tension Arc

A participant gives a presentation or tells a story. The audience members raise their hands when the tension subsides. In this way, the presenter receives immediate feedback about the tension arc of their presentation or story.

Exercise

Half-Time Presentation

Two players go together into breakout sessions and give their presentation. Then, they deliver it again in half of the original time and then in the next round in half the time again. This pattern continues until the presentation consists of only one sentence.

TECHNOLOGY

- Breakout sessions: partner work

Exercise

Director

As part of this exercise in high status, the participants will briefly welcome all the others present. This is in the role of a director/managing director of the university/company, etc. Afterwards, the participants just addressed raise a green or red sheet – green if the greeting was convincing; red if it was rather less convincing.

Exercise

Call-Out Presentation

The audience sets a theme, and the player improvises a short presentation. In the course of the lecture, the audience calls out key words, which should be incorporated into the presentation as soon as possible. This trains the ability to handle spontaneous inputs skilfully.

TECHNOLOGY

- All participants switch to speaker view.
- The players can change their camera settings if they want so that they do not see themselves.

Exercise

Role-Playing Dealing with Criticism

The player is given a theme for their presentation (e.g. horses – but the player can't choose). The game starts with the player thanking the audience and opening a question and answer session. Then, someone from the audience asks a critical question or makes a critical remark. Now, the presenter tries to answer this question with an internal "Yes, and . . . " response. The audience, and especially the critics, give feedback afterwards on how the presenter handled the criticism.

Exercise

Elevator Pitch

Within the duration of an elevator ride, the participants have to introduce their own work to someone. This exercise is performed in pairs: one person presents their idea to another person in a maximum of one minute. Beforehand, it can be determined who the counterpart is, for example, a possible sponsor, a potential contractee and a potential customer.

Afterwards, feedback is given on what was more convincing and what was less so.

TECHNOLOGY

- All spectators turn off their cameras so that only the players are visible. To do this, all participants must select "Hide Non-Video Participantso" in their video settings.

Chapter 6

Practical examples

Online workshop: "Good cooperation in difficult times"
Austrian Research Promotion Agency (FFG) in cooperation
with the University of Natural Resources and Life Sciences,
Vienna (BOKU)

Key points

Institutions

The **Austrian Research Promotion Agency** (FFG) is the national
funding agency for business-related research and development in
Austria. It runs the w-fFORTE programme on behalf of the Federal
Ministry for Digital and Economic Affairs. w-fFORTE supports the
vision of greater equity of opportunity and wants to make more
women visible in key roles in research and innovation in the region.

The **University of Natural Resources and Life Sciences, Vienna**
(BOKU), on the other hand, is a teaching and research institute dedicated to the management of natural resources. A special feature of the
university is the combination of natural sciences, technology and social
sciences and economics. The continuous development of leadership
and gender competences in the scientific business is a central concern
of BOKU, while the large range of training courses offered by the
Department of Personnel Development is a sign of this commitment.

Event

An online workshop is to strengthen the ability to interact with others in projects and cross-disciplinary cooperation. The innovative
and experimental methods of applied improvisation are intended

DOI: 10.4324/9781003172765-6

to explore subtleties in cooperation and communication that are not normally discussed.

Duration

From 9:00 a.m. to 10:30 a.m. from Monday to Friday (five days)

Target group

Researchers from cooperative or application-oriented research and companies, which were able to participate through the w-fFORTE programme, and BOKU researchers

Goals

The participants . . .

- practise active presence and attention.
- learn how to make their colleagues "look good."
- refine their ability to recognise and accept so-called "offers."
- expand their status flexibility and thus the ability to work together on an equal footing.
- increase their flexibility and spontaneity and thus their ability to be creative in communication.
- experience important basic attitudes for the emergence of innovation.

The aim was to strengthen exchange and networking between women from different organisations and disciplines from science and business.

Starting point

In April 2020, a face-to-face workshop for the w-fFORTE programme in cooperation with BOKU in Vienna was planned. Since this was cancelled due to corona lockdown, the idea arose to offer a virtual workshop. Expanded to include the current issues and challenges of the situation, the workshop was held online in May 2020 via videoconference (Zoom), in a women-only group. Session times were Monday to Friday from 9:00 a.m. to

10:30 p.m. The short-time blocks spread over five days worked very well, as did the setting up of a Slack Channel (Slack is a cloud-based collaboration application) through which the participants communicated further with each other and received preparatory tasks for the next day's session. In this way, the participants were able to try out what they had learned on the same day in their professional cooperation, apply it and also do some networking.

Why applied improvisation?

Applied improvisation is a method that is now successfully used in many companies and institutions around the world. The principles and methods from improvisational theatre are used and adapted for other fields, for example, training and consulting. Many social skills that have become even more important in today's often unpredictable times, such as agility, creativity, teamwork and status flexibility (collaboration on an equal footing), can be learned and improved with these techniques.

Successful communication is a key to success in researchers' collaboration across organisational and discipline boundaries and – in international projects – across geographic boundaries. However, this is easily lost in everyday project work with different partners from different research, working cultures and varied personality types. Instead of cooperation and building bridges between disciplines or organisations, work tends to be done "in parallel" and in the form of work packages.

In particular through the status exercises, discipline- or gender-specific communication behaviour, which may have been learned by socialisation as a man or woman or in the respective field of science or research, can become visible and thus intentionally addressed.

Content

In face-to-face situations – and even more so under the difficult conditions of purely online interaction, in which unconscious communication channels such as body language are only available to a limited extent – good cooperation is characterised above all by listening to each other, making other team members look good, as well as picking up ideas and developing them further.

The so-called "Yes, and . . . " principle is essential for the development of innovative solutions. The first step is to open up a creative space that allows the spontaneous and uncensored emergence of ideas, thoughts, associations, analogies, images, etc. This is supported by an explicit "Yes, and . . . " response to ideas and by the fact that the contributions of the colleagues are taken as inspiration, carried forward and further developed. This interplay can create unexpected, surprising new solutions and cross-divisional cooperation, the results of which extend "outside the box."

This type of cooperation on an equal footing is essentially based on the clarity of the parties concerned about their own status behaviour. Lowering one's own status, for example, and thereby increasing that of the other person conveys empathy and sympathy. On the other hand, a high status enhances assertiveness. Both are important and necessary in various situations of productive cooperation.

In addition to the basic collaboration skills described, another goal was to promote the joy of co-creation even in uncertain times and to discover that targeted cooperation is also very possible online.

Procedure

Preparatory task on Slack

I asked the participants to introduce themselves personally and professionally in the Slack room and to talk about their expectations for the workshop.

Monday

Monday was dedicated to the topics of "getting to know each other" and "accepting offers." In the online workshop, the "getting to know each other" round took place, with the exercise "What Else Would I Have Liked to Become" (see p. 43). The aim of this exercise is to lead the participants into a different, creative world and to leave their usual professional life outside as much as possible.

I led the topic "accepting offers" with the "No – yes, but . . . – yes, and . . . " exercise (see p. 24). This exercise makes it clear when it is appropriate to accept offers and when a strong "no" is more fitting. The "Yes, and . . . " principle as the basis of co-creative work becomes clear and tangible.

Breakout sessions

I ended the first day of the course with an exchange in small groups on the question of what experiences the participants had had so far with blockades and the topic of "accepting offers."

Preparatory task on Slack

Throughout the rest of today, count how often you say "no," "yes, but," "yes, and." How often do I hear "no," "yes, but" "yes, and"? What happens next? What happens if I say "yes, and"? Write a short report in the Slack Channel.

Tuesday

Tuesday started with association exercises (see pp. 29-31). These make it possible to say "yes, and . . . " to our own impulses and to suppress our own internal censor. The day also deepened the topic of accepting offers with the exercises "Giving Gifts" (see p. 29) and "Who Can Accept Offers Better" (see p. 27). Based on the exercise "One-sentence Stories" (see p. 65), I introduced the topic of storytelling. Short inputs on my part on the topics "making your partner look good" (see p. 3) and "storytelling" complemented the sequence.

Breakout sessions

The task in the small groups was to think about current difficult situations that had to do with the topic of accepting offers and to discuss them together.

Preparatory task on Slack

Introduce yourself on Slack with the highest possible status – list all your titles and achievements!

Wednesday

At the beginning of the day, I asked the participants how easy or difficult it had been to introduce themselves, in writing, with such a high status. As expected, many participants had felt certain inhibitions, and it was very revealing to briefly discuss the reasons for that. The theme "status" was then deepened with the following exercises: "Status Appearance" (see p. 76), "Status Meeting" (see p. 79) and "Status Battles" (see p. 78). It is important to emphasise here that high-status behaviour is no better than low-status behaviour and that status flexibility can support good cooperation on an equal footing.

Breakout sessions

The following questions were to be discussed in the small groups:

- How do you experience the topic of status in your everyday life?
- What status do you feel most comfortable with yourself?

Preparatory task on Slack

Put pictures of public figures with very high or very low status in the Slack Channel for tomorrow.

Thursday

On Thursday, the participants presented their photos from the preparatory task. In two groups, they then collected tricky current conversation situations and then introduced one of these situations in a role-play. All participants then went over this together (see improvised role-playing games, pp. 48-49) by discussing the situation and giving feedback to the person contributing the case in question. As soon as someone made a suggestion about how else to behave in this situation, that person slipped into the role of the person bringing the case and tried it themselves. The group then gave feedback. Work was mainly done on the themes of "accepting offers," "making the partner look good" and "status behaviour." In the end, the person bringing the case had several solutions available for their situation.

Preparatory task on Slack

On the Slack Channel, place photos of people who positively impress you with their status behaviour and briefly describe how they do that.

Friday

On the last day of the course, each participant was able to present their photos. Then, we worked on the role-playing game from the second group from the previous day and concluded the day with a review of the whole workshop.

Completion feedback on Slack

In the end, the participants also submitted written feedback via the Slack Channel.

Benefits for the participants

The participants described the benefits of the workshop on Slack as follows:

- *The workshop identified new aspects that contribute to efficiency in communication and have a supportive effect. Not only on the recipient, but also on ourselves (status, body language). The exercises performed were very clear, with an immediate learning effect.*

- *The workshop supported self-reflection and showed new solutions in conflict situations.*
- *Very helpful topics that allow a new approach to many meetings and conversations. The desire to improvise and try things out is awakened, and the horizon is expanded.*
- *The workshop was very helpful and enriching for communication in the workplace and private life (and with yourself)!*
- *The workshop made me think about how often women are taught a certain body language from an early age, which lowers their status, and how much this body language also influences self-criticism.*

Customer feedback from Andrea Handsteiner (Head of Human Resources Development BOKU) and Charlotte Alber (Programme Manager for w-fFORTE in the FFG):

"W-fFORTE has been working for many years for the promotion of women, which is necessary for successful collaboration in cooperative or application-oriented research. Gender-specific training is also a major concern at BOKU, a science and technology-oriented university. When attempting to deepen collaboration skills, classical training methods often only skim the surface, or remain very theoretical, on the meta level. Applied Improvisation actively reveals unspoken challenges from everyday project life. The method thus leads to rapid learning and effective self-reflection of behavioural patterns. What is exciting is the co-creative attitude required. Especially in the innovation environment, the 'Yes, and!' and the willingness to 'quickly succeed through rapid failure' is central to developing new ideas and perspectives. It has been shown during the training that this attitude towards innovation – whose methods may look playful from the outside – has a lasting strengthening effect.

The improvisation exercises go beyond tried-and-tested role-playing games and enable direct learning from experience. For this reason, we always offer workshops that cover important cooperation and communication topics with applied improvisation. The first workshop in 2018 (also a cooperation between w-fFORTE and BOKU) was offered in a mixed-gender setting in order to put gender-specific behaviour patterns on the table. In subsequent sessions, women-only groups have proved particularly successful: in this learning setting, there is a greater tendency to reflect on situations openly. In the feedback, an 'a-ha effect' is often noticeable: A-ha, others feel the same way – and you can make everyday professional situations even more effective by using flexible status. The far-reaching networking effect was also surprising: in the w-fFORTE network, a self-organised peer group (people with similar backgrounds and goals) has been formed, which meets regularly (also online) and works on professional situations with improv methods, as well as another peer group, which exchanges ideas on new projects in the field of the 17 SDGs (Sustainable Development Goals from the '2030 Agenda for Sustainable Development' of the United Nations).

The COVID-19 pandemic in particular has shown that we need every single researcher to work on the major challenges. Research and innovation offer encouragement to people, and foster confidence in our future. That is why it was important for us to have the workshop – originally planned as a classroom event – carried out online. It was an exciting experience for everyone and showed that Applied Improvisation is such a viable method that it works very well online too!"

Online workshop: "Status behaviour and status flexibility"
AIT – Austrian Institute of Technology

Key points

Institution

Among European research institutes, the AIT – Austrian Institute of Technology, Austria's largest non-university research institute, is a specialist in the key infrastructure issues of the future. In Austria, there are over 1,100 staff members working on the development of those tools, technologies and solutions for Austrian industry considered to be of relevance for the future and which comply with the institute's motto "Tomorrow Today."

Mission

The AIT wants to at least maintain – or ideally increase – the relatively low proportion of women in its workforce. To achieve this, the institute wishes to strengthen and foster its female staff.

For this purpose, it makes sense, among other things, to professionalise the way women appear in the organisation. For example, their appearance as competent and self-confident cooperation partners on an equal footing is to be promoted through a better perception of their own status behaviour and a higher status flexibility.

Duration

Two days from 9:00 a.m. to 5:00 p.m. – the first day's workshop held in German and the second day's workshop in English.

Target group

2 × 14 AIT scientists and researchers

Goals

The participants . . .

- get to know their preferred status.
- learn to more easily change their status and adapt it to the situation, increasing their status flexibility.
- get to know the different ways status is communicated (body language, speech and the use of space and time) and learn to perceive and use them more consciously.
- increase their spontaneity and expand the range of their individual expressive abilities (personal authenticity).
- learn to be more assertive and appear more professional when dealing with unpleasant situations.

Content

The aim of this workshop was to help the participants get to know their own status better, especially in exchanges with male colleagues. Participants practised working on their own status flexibility, to be able to adjust their status according to the situation. They learned how to consciously expand the range of their status behaviour and to actively deploy it.

The aim was to help women at AIT to be self-confident and effective in how they present themselves and for them to be able to make their voices heard and their interests and positions clearer in difficult, gender-specific situations.

Procedure

On the basis of getting to know each other and a series of preparatory exercises in the "Yes, and . . . " principle and status flexibility, working with this group focused on experimenting with the dynamics and typical situations of everyday life.

In the afternoon, the participants were given the following task for joint group work in breakout sessions:

- How do you experience the theme of status in your everyday life?
- What would you like to try out?
- Think of difficult conversation situations and note them on Padlet (a digital pinboard).
- Then select a challenging situation and prepare a role-playing game (the person bringing the case plays herself).

Difficult situations with both male and female colleagues could be prepared.

Here is a selection of the situations recorded on Padlet:

- *After a lecture an older gentleman comes to me, and tells me – in front of a group of (unfamiliar) professional partners that I definitely get the "prize for the most attractive lecturer."*
- *Transmitting high status, but also staying sympathetic is difficult. Fear of annoying high-status colleagues.*
- *Talking to "older," more experienced colleagues/superiors, it is hard to step out of low status.*
- *Knowing what you're talking about, but still coming across as uncertain. A quiet/weak voice does not underline the fact that you know the subject well.*
- *Professional and formal competence is questioned by more inexperienced colleagues who are preferred by the boss.*

In the role-playing game, among other things, the first situation after the lecture was dealt with: The woman who contributed the case role-played the situation together with a colleague from her group. (Technology: everyone else turns off their camera and selects "Hide Non-Video Participantso.")

After initial feedback, suggestions were quickly made as to how to behave in this situation. Here, I asked those offering a suggestion to play it out, rather than just explaining the approach. The participant in question then took on the role of the one bringing the case and replayed the situation. In this way, several possible approaches were gradually created within the framework of the original situation. In the end, the original contributor spoke again about which new perspectives and solutions she would take into her work.

In this role-playing game, various possible reactions were played out:

- Neutral: *"Aha – and what did you think about my talk?"*
- Charming: *"Intelligent and attractive – indeed, that wouldn't be a bad combination. But are you also attracted to what I was saying?"*
- Humour: *"My appearance threw you off? Perhaps, after this initial shock, can you say what you think of the content of my speech?"*
- Fighting talk: *"Since we are not running a beauty contest here, I would be solely interested in whether and to what extent you agree with my remarks."*
- Direct: *"Please accept that I do not wish to receive feedback on my appearance. Instead, focus on the content of my presentation."*

Customer feedback from Beatrix Wepner (Scientist, Center for Innovation Systems & Policy, AIT) and Ursula Sauer (Chair of the AIT Works Council):

"The increase in the proportion of women, especially in management positions, is still an issue at the AIT as well as in the technology research industry in general. One aspect of the problem is the so-called 'leaky pipeline': while the proportion of women entering the profession is still around 30%, this proportion decreases as careers progress. As the AIT works council, we strive to understand the many causes of this development and to counteract them accordingly. The organisation of training courses for women, together with management, is one of the measures. The workshop on status flexibility not only gave the participants some a-ha moments and new insights, and the opportunity to practise, but was also visibly fun. In addition, the workshop also met a desire for more networking among the colleagues, and a group for further joint activities was subsequently formed. The management decided to include the subject in the training catalogue, not least because of the positive feedback from the participants. Despite the online format, a valuable contribution to the empowerment and networking of women in the AIT was achieved."

Online large group event:
Internal training for teachers from the city schools in Zug, Switzerland
Zug Department of Education

Key points

Institution

The Herti and Letzi school complex consists of several school buildings and kindergartens, run jointly by co-headteachers as a school unit. Around 550 pupils from kindergarten to 6th year are taught by about 70 teachers. The Herti–Letzi School Unit is a public elementary school and belongs to the Zug City Schools.

Over 2,300 pupils, from kindergarten to upper secondary school, as well as the remedial school, attend classes at the Zug City Schools.

Mission

Internal training to help the teachers improve their ability to cooperate with the students, parents and colleagues. On the one hand, by learning to accept offers more consciously and to build on them. On the other hand, the workshop aimed to strengthen participants' individual ability to promote and deepen exchanges with each other through adapted status behaviour and authoritative presentation.

In addition, the participants would learn about various interactive exercises and methods that they can use in their online lessons.

Duration

One day from 9:00 a.m. to 4:30 p.m.

Target group

68 teachers

Goals

The participants . . .

- learn the "Yes, and . . . " principle as the key to engaging and motivating cooperation.
- learn to use body language more consciously in the classroom.
- learn about their own status behaviour in communication with students, parents and colleagues and how to change it more easily if necessary.
- compare experiences with each other and learn from each other.
- expand their room for manoeuvre in unexpected situations and in difficult conversations.
- learn different interactive exercises and methods for their own online lessons.

Content

At the beginning of the training day, the "Yes, and . . . " principle as a basis for good cooperation was introduced. Good cooperation not only in the team but also with the students and parents is characterised by the fact that the participants listen to each other and take each other seriously. They take up ideas and suggestions, carry them on and thus lay a basis for real cooperation on an equal footing. It is both a matter of participants' saying "yes, and . . . " to their own ideas, as well as welcoming and building on the wishes of colleagues, students and parents. Through cooperation between all parties, jointly developed solutions will be supported by all.

Clarity about one's own status behaviour is crucial for successful cooperation. Lowering one's own status and thus increasing the status of the other person conveys empathy and sympathy. On the other hand, high status can support assertiveness. Both are important and helpful in different situations in school collaboration.

In this training, the focus was on the ability of the teachers to cooperate and the joy of developing common solutions.

Procedure

The workshop was originally planned as a face-to-face training event in Zug but had to be changed to an online format because of corona. I put together a model group of six volunteers for each unit. First, all 68 participants turned off their cameras and selected "Hide Non-Video Participantso." Then, I asked for six volunteers to turn on their cameras and be available as my model group until the break.

With this model group, I demonstrated the exercises and then evaluated them. I only allowed questions from the model group, assuming that they would be representative of the whole group and that other questions could be answered later in the subsequent breakout sessions.

After the exercises in breakout sessions, all 68 participants deactivated their cameras again and I resumed working with the model group. After each break, I invited a new model group, so that as many participants as possible could be actively involved and seen.

The programme for the day looked like this:

09:00–09:15	Welcome, presentation and start-up
09:15–10:30	Theme: Accepting offers – interactive lecture and exercises
10:30–10:50	*Coffee break*
10:50–11:30	Group work: Reflection and transfer
11:30–12:00	Reports from the groups
12:00–12:30	Theme: Status – interactive lecture and exercises
12:30–13:30	*Lunch break*
13:30–15:00	Continuation of theme: Status – interactive lecture and exercises
15:00–15:20	*Coffee break*
15:20–15:50	Group work: Reflection and transfer
15:50–16:15	Reports and reflection on role-playing games from the groups
16:15–16:30	Conclusion

To get started and for everyone to get to know each other, I chose the exercise "What Else Would I Have Liked to Become" (see p. 43). This exercise is very suitable if some of the participants already know each other. I demonstrated the exercise with two volunteers from my model group, then got all participants to do the exercise in breakout sessions, in groups of six.

After exercises for the "Yes, and . . . " principle and the first break, I began with the exercise "Finding Things in Common" (see p. 43). To do this, all participants must first turn off their cameras, and one participant starts by turning on their camera and saying something about themselves, for example, "*I like to travel*" or "*I have a cat.*" All participants to whom the statement applies then also turn on their camera, and similarities start to become clear. This exercise is also suitable for large groups.

After the break, I continued with the topic status. With my model group, I also demonstrated the exercise "Good Evening Ladies and Gentlemen" (see "Status Appearance," p. 76), where the participants could choose their status number from 1 to 10. Afterwards, I got all the teachers do the exercise in breakout sessions, in groups of six.

In the afternoon, the focus was the status paradox of Maike Plath, which was illustrated and deepened in real situations from everyday school life in the form of role-playing games. The group chose two situations:

1   A teacher asks the students to collect balls and bring them back. One student refuses and throws a ball at the teacher's feet.
2   A parent storms into the classroom during a lesson and shouts at the teacher about their child being bullied by the class.

In the first situation, Maike Plath's status paradox proved its worth. Of course, it's very tempting for the teacher to jump straight into high status and try to get the child to pick up the ball again. But in doing so, the teacher risks someone losing face: either their own if the child refuses, or that of the child, if the child has to bend before the teacher in front of the whole class to pick up the ball again.

Another technique worked on together was remaining calm and confident within (high status inside) but assuming a lower status outwardly and asking the child how he or she is experiencing this situation. With that, the attention shifts from the ball towards the child and thus the focus of interest to where it really belongs ("Yes, and ... " principle).

In the second situation, it was possible to work out with the help of role-playing how important it is to avoid a high-status fight in front of an interested audience and not going into attack or defence mode. Participants saw that it is vital to immediately ask about the concern, to listen and understand the situation. Of course, clarifying the situation before the class would be inappropriate – if at all possible, given that the affected parent is clearly emotionally out of control. Here, the mother or father therefore needs guidance via high-status behaviour on the part of the teacher. A useful approach would be, for example, that the teacher does not let herself or himself lose composure and leaves the classroom – the parent has to follow, and a proper meeting can then be arranged outside the classroom.

Client feedback by Sandra Hürlimann (Head of School/ Education Department Zug)

"The topic of status competence and status flexibility is central to teachers. They work with students on a daily basis, plan their lessons with colleagues, meet to exchange ideas on school and teaching development, and have discussions with parents and care services. Where there is a lot of talk and discussion, misunderstandings can occur. Communication is a demanding topic and places significant strain on us in everyday life. That is why we wanted use to training to deal with this, together with the subject of managing conversations and the personal impact on others.

Due to corona, it was not possible to hold the event as planned. Just like improvisational theatre, the theme of status and performance competence thrives on encounters between people. That's why addressing this subject online was very strange to us at first. In a preliminary discussion, Susanne Schinko-Fischli showed us (the co-heads of Herti-Letzi) in detail how she works with Zoom. Suddenly, in the new situation of delivering further education online, we could also see advantages, and additional learning opportunities. In addition to the training's main focus on the subject of status and performance competence, the teachers also became more familiar with the online tool, with its many possible applications. We know these platforms from the time of distance learning; however, an event of this size was a novelty for everyone.

The evaluation of the training has shown that the main areas of content got through to all participants. When giving feedback, the teachers had to indicate their personal learning gain, new knowledge, and how they may transfer it into practice. The 'Yes, and...' principle, status behaviour, status flexibility, body language and also the positive experience with digital training were mentioned by almost everyone.

This workshop showed how the methods of applied improvisation are also suitable online to impart and practise social skills. The way the breakout groups were quickly assembled, and the exchanges that happened in those groups, were particularly appreciated. Susanne Schinko-Fischli's interesting specialist inputs, leadership and clear instructions and exercises all contributed to the success of this training. We were surprised to find that it is completely viable to work interactively with such a large group online, to learn so much, and to have a lot of fun doing it!"

Your takeaways from this book

- Online workshops can promote and meaningfully support the training of social skills if the opportunities for presence events are limited or unavailable for whatever reason.
- Conflict and crisis interventions as well as workshops in the field of personality, team and organisational development should be conducted at least partially, or if possible exclusively, in face-to-face workshops.
- Applied improvisation is also an excellent way to teach social skills interactively and playfully online.
- In order for us to be able to collaborate co-creatively online, a certain bond and a basic trust must be built up. For this, it is important to apply the "Yes, and . . . " principle to take up ideas and to develop them together, as well as to be able to fail with good humour.
- Storytelling as a method can also be used online very well in order to convey knowledge in a practical, exciting and emotional way. In addition, stories and so-called Hero's Journeys can be used to improve teamwork.
- Status games also take place online! This makes it all the more important to be aware of one's own status behaviour and to be able to adapt one's own status to the situation.

Literature

Adams, K. (2007). *How to improvise a full-length play – The art of spontaneous theater*. New York: Allworth.

Cossart, E. V. (2015). *Story tells – Story sells*. 3rd ed. Bergisch-Gladbach: Lesedrehbuch.

Edmondson, A. (2013). *Teaming to innovate*. San Francisco: Bass & Wiley.

Johnstone, K. (1979). IMPRO: *Improvisation and the theatre*. London: Methuen Publishing.

Johnstone, K. (1998). *Impro for storytellers*. London: Faber and Faber Limited.

Lehner, J. M., and Ötsch, W. O. (2015). *Jenseits der Hierarchie – Status im beruflichen Alltag aktiv gestalten* (Beyond hierarchy – Shaping status actively in everyday professional life). 2nd ed. Weinheim: Wiley-VCH.

Leonard, K., and Yorton, T. (2015). *Yes, and – Lessons from the second city*. New York: Collins.

Plath, M. (2015). *Spielend unterrichten und Kommunikation gestalten* (Playful teaching and communication). 2nd ed. Weinheim and Basel: Beltz Verlag.

Salinsky, T. (2020). *The power of storytelling – A seminar from the spontaneity shop*.

Schinko-Fischli, S. (2019). *Applied improvisation for coaches and leaders*. Abingdon: Routledge.

Online sources

Beglinger,M.(2013).*DerStaatderPhysiker(Cern)*.DasMagazin.Retrieved30.3.2021. www.dasmagazin.ch/2013/10/25/der-staat-der-physiker/?reduced=true.

Duhigg, C. (2016). *What Google learned from its Quest to build the perfect team*. New York Times. Retrieved 31.8.2021. www.nytimes.com/2016/02/28/magazine/what-google-learned-from-its-quest-to-build-the-perfect-team.html

Mordrelle, E. (2020). *Warum das Homeoffice unsere Jobs bedroht* (Why home office is threatening our jobs). Tagesanzeiger. Retrieved 30.3.2021. www.tagesanzeiger.ch/warum-das-homeoffice-unsere-jobs-bedroht-402635704764.

Index

accepting offers 24–29; first round 25; second round 25; technology 26; third round 25

Adams, Kenn 53

agility, creativity and 18–24; commitment 19–20; courage 23–24; focus 20; improvisation 19–24; openness 20–22; respect 22–23; Scrum 19

appearance online 74–76; background 75; Call-Out Presentation exercise 82; camera 74; Director exercise 81; Elevator Pitch exercise 82; exercises for 80–83; eye contact 75; "eye-to-eye" level 74; feedback on online presence 75–76; Half-Time Presentation exercise 81; image framing 74; lighting 74; PowerPoint Karaoke exercise 76; presence 75; Role-Playing Dealing with Criticism exercise 82; Tension Arc exercise 81

applied improvisation 1–11; need for 86; Playback Theatre 1; in teamwork 37; Theatre of the Oppressed 1; *see also* online workshops in applied improvisation

Applied Improvisation for Coaches and Leaders 2

Applied Improvisation Network (AIN) 1; basic principles 2–3; here-and-now principle 2–3; making your partner look good 3; methods of 2; "Yes, and . . . " – accepting offers 3

associations 29–33

Austrian Institute of Technology (AIT) 91–92

Austrian Research Promotion Agency (FFG) 84

"Birthday Messages" exercise 20, 32

Boal, Augusto 1

building stories 53–57; beginning 54–55; climax introducing solution 55; consequences shown 55; end establishing new routine 55–57; event breaking the routine 55; "Story Spine" 53–54, **53;** structure of a story 54; tension increased 55

Campbell, Joseph 59

chat 6–7

(co-)creativity 12–16; failing with good humour 15–16; ideas, separating generation and evaluation of 14; online role-playing game 15; prerequisites 12; "What Comes Next" exercise 13

commitment 19–20

constructive online meetings 40–42; Destruction rule 1, Block 40; Destruction rule 2, Apparent consent 40–41; Destruction rule 3, Be negative 41; Destruction rule 4, Duck out 41; Destruction rule 5, Dodge or distract 41–42; Destruction rule 6, Gags 42; Destruction rule 7, Don't let others influence you 42

content 86–87
convergent thinking 17
Cossart, E. V. 53
courage 23–24
creativity 12–33; analysis phase 18;
    brainstorming phase 18; convergent
    thinking 17; divergent thinking 17;
    evaluation and selection phase 18;
    implementation phase 18;
    online 16–17; phases of 17–18;
    see also agility, creativity and;
    (co-)creativity
creativity online, exercises for 24–33;
    visual thinking 31; "Yes, and . . ."
    principle–accept offers 24–29;
    see also accepting offers
critical feedback 48–49

destruction rules 40
digital storytelling 52–53
divergent thinking 17

Edmondson, Amy 36
emotions in teamwork online 39
event 84–85

face-to-face versus online workshops
    10–11
feedback on online presence 75–76
"Finding Things in Common"
    exercise 43
focus 20
"Follow the Leader" exercise 45
Fox, Jonathan 1

"Genre Object" exercise 30
"Giving Gifts" exercise 29
Guilford, Joy Paul 17

here-and-now principle 2–3
Hero's Journey 59–60; offline,
    managers 61; online, team
    development 60–61; performance
    skills 61–62; using 60–62
hierarchy paradox 73–74
high status behaviour 67–68
high status online 71
"Hit Lucas" exercise 45
"Hollywood Swing" exercise 21, 26

"I Am a Tree" exercise 31
ideas, generation and evaluation of,
    separating 14
image framing 74
improvisation 1–11; see also applied
    improvisation
improvisational theatre, origin 1
improvised role-playing games online
    48–49
informal chat 38

Jackson, Paul Z. 1–2
Johnstone, Keith 1, 13, 40, 66
Joyce, James 15

"Last Word/First Word" exercise 46
Lehner, J. M. 74
Leonard, Kelly 23
low-status behaviour 66–68
low-status online 71
Lucas, George 59

Macron, Emmanuel 67
message of stories 57–59
Moreno, Jacob Levy 1

"No – yes, but . . . – yes, and . . . "
    exercise 24

"One-sentence Story" exercise 20
"One-Word Stories" exercise 46
online storytelling 52–53; building
    stories 63–65; exercises for 62–65;
    Increasing the Risk 64; My Hero's
    Journey 62; One-Sentence Stories
    65; stories of collaboration 65;
    stories of the participants 62–63;
    Story, Colour, Emotion 64; Story
    Spine 63; Three-Sentence
    Stories 64
online workshops in applied
    improvisation 4–11; chat 6–7;
    disadvantage 6; experimenting
    online 9–10; face-to-face versus
    10–11; interaction, camera and
    microphone on 5–6; large groups 9;
    participant versus host centring 7;
    PowerPoint slides 7; script 8; social
    online learning 11; technology 5

openness 20–22, 39
Ötsch, W. O. 74

Padlet 5, 93
Pasteur, Louis 15
personal chat 38
PowerPoint Karaoke exercise 76
practical examples 84–99
"Press Conference" exercise 47
psychological security in
    teamwork 35–36

respect 22–23
Rosenburg, Michael 2
Rostain, Alain 2
Rowling, J. K. 59

Salinsky, Tom 52, 57
script 8
Scrum method 19
Slack Channel 86–87; benefits for
    the participants 89–92; completion
    feedback on 89; preparatory task
    on 87–89
"Speed Dating" exercise 44
"Spontaneity Shop, The" theatre
    group 52
starting point 85–86
status: behaviour 66–69; flexibility
    68–69; high 67; and image 66–83;
    low 66; paradox 73; in sales 69;
    and women 69
status online 69–73; exercises for
    76–80; Guessing Status exercise
    79; high-status online 71; low-
    status online 71; online meetings
    69; online workshops 69; status
    and space 72; status and time
    72–73; Status Appearance exercise
    76; Status Battles exercise 78;
    status behaviour online 70; Status
    Feedback exercise 77; Status
    Meeting exercise 79; Status See-saw
    exercise 78; videoconferencing 69
"Story Spine" 53–54, **53**, 56
storytelling 50–65; colour 57; creativity
    in *51*; elements 57; emotion 57;
    Hero's Journey 59–60; message
    of stories 57–59; online 52–53;

online, exercises for 62–65; story
    57; *see also* building stories; Hero's
    Journey; online storytelling
Strohm, Oliver 17

teamwork 34–49; applied
    improvisation in 37; cooperation
    34; critical feedback 48–49;
    difficult conversational situations
    49; exchange and transfer 47–48;
    exercises for 42–48; getting to
    know each other 43–44; improvised
    role-playing games online 48–49;
    leading and letting to be led 37,
    46–48; movement and activation
    exercises 45; prerequisites for 36;
    psychological security 35–36; "Yes,
    and . . . " principle in a team 45–46
teamwork online 37–42; clear decisions,
    making 40; clear structure in 40;
    emotions, show and acknowledge
    39; explicit instead of implicit
    39; informal chat 38; openness
    39; personal chat 38; *see also*
    constructive online meetings
"Two Truths" exercise 44

University of Natural Resources and
    Life Sciences, Vienna (BOKU), 84

visual thinking 31
Vogler, Christoph 59

"Walk and Talk" exercise 47
w-fFORTE programme 84–85, 90
"What Comes Next?" exercise 28
"What Else Would I Have Liked to
    Become?" exercise 43
"Who Can Accept Offers Better?"
    exercise 27
"Who Can Block Offers Better?"
    exercise 27

"Yes and – Lessons from The Second
    City" 23
"Yes, and . . . " principle in a team 45–46
Yorton, Tom 23

"Zoom" videoconferencing 5, 9

Printed in the United States
by Baker & Taylor Publisher Services